With best wishes —

George D. Mullen

George D. Mullen, **President**
GLOBAL DIPLOMACY THINK TANK
Box 2806 Del Mar, CA 92014

PEACE
In The
Middle East

A Realistic Proposal for Ending the
Israeli—Palestinian Conflict

PRINTED IN THE UNITED STATES OF AMERICA
-by-
ICAN PRESS
616 THIRD AVENUE
CHULA VISTA, CA 91910

FIRST EDITION

Peace in the Middle East

A Realistic Proposal for Ending the Israeli-Palestinian Conflict

-by-

George D. Mullen

San Diego, California
June 1994
First Edition

Printed in the United States of America
Library of Congress
Cataloging-in-Publication Data
ISBN: 1-881116-46-8

For those who deserve most a future based
on peace . . . the children.

Foreword

What one world event could lessen the daily stress and tension around the globe today? What single happening could be a catalyst for bringing security and safety to millions of people? What occurrence could possibly allow disgruntled followers of different religions to work and live side-by-side, without any fear of personal attack? What would permit diametrically opposed cultures to flourish and grow without being inhibited or held back by the other? The basic answer is simple, but the solution is much more complex. Author George Mullen discusses the intrinsic and inner thoughts of two peoples and their quest for equality and acceptance—the subject is a workable Middle East Peace Proposal.

The personal ideas expressed by Mr. Mullen, in *Peace in the Middle East,* are very thoroughly and carefully prepared and well thought out. His words are not empty and must not fall on deaf ears, as his outline for peace is founded on knowledge, first-hand experience and true facts concerning Arabs and Jews. His proposal is comprehensive, workable and fair—it is a win-win compromise; however, it will take considerable work and a significant amount of dedicated effort by both Israelis and Palestinians.

Religious leaders may view such a peace proposal as prophetic—perhaps it is, but the concerns of most Jewish and Islamic holy leaders will be focused on whether or not the two faiths can successfully assimilate by unconditionally respecting what the other faith peacefully professes. The greatest clashes so far have been over whose god, Allah or Jehovah, gave land rights to—and who is more blessed and deserving—the children of Jacob or the children of Ishmael. Both Jew and Arab have a claim to the land and a right to exist and be free. Most of the democratic world heartily agrees.

Initially, peace must be resolved with a mutually acceptable treaty, beneficial to both Palestinian and Israeli. It must be just, perhaps a covenant supported by the Heads of State, and/or a third unbiased party. The world would soon experience new Middle East leadership because of the continuous testing of this treaty through it transitional stages, but peaceful implementations will be demanded.

If Mr. Mullen's peace proposal was, in fact, used as the blueprint to secure and restore peace to the land of Abraham, its framework would facilitate relative ease in change. However easy the changes would be, it may produce a forced peace settlement—old wounds take time to heal. Israel may have to reluctantly part with the territories of Gaza and the West Bank, land conquered through war. And to get Israel to do this will be difficult, Jewish leaders will probably demand, for an exchange of land, exceptionally strong international and Arab guarantees of Israel's safety and future prosperity. *Peace in the Middle East* addresses this issue sensibly with reason and sensitivity—it penetrates the core of this debate.

Peace in the Middle East directly faces the most controversial issues while providing realistic solutions to them. Those issues include the efficacy of land for peace, statehood for the Palestinians, the status of Jerusalem, the Jewish settlers in the occupied territories, and the importance of security to both communities. Both Jew and Arab want peace, both want their own sovereignty and freedom to prosper—their only solution will come if peaceful co-existence terms are detailed in an acceptable treaty. So far only one-sided peace proposals have been offered; little compromise or "give and take" has ever reached the table. It is time to get real and deal with the facts—those that work and not those that won't. This text cleverly expounds upon those facts, ways, and means that will work. But both sides must be willing to seek agreement more than disagreement.

ii

The text of this book is very simply written, it is easy to read, follow and understand. There are no complexities built-in to Mr. Mullen's ideas, only a clear streamlined roadmap for peace . . . ideas and suggestions gleaned from the people of the Middle East themselves.

This is a proposal which can work—I hope it is taken into serious consideration. God meant this earth to be shared, for men to be free and for fairness and justice to prevail. The nation of Israel and the people of Palestine must give peace a chance—they both must diligently and sincerely seek compromise.

George Mullen has provided a workable outline, a guide to real Middle East peace—I commend his wisdom and insight. May it work!

Dahk Knox, Ed.D., Ph.D.
April, 1994

Table of Contents

Foreward i

Preface ix

Chapter 1 1
An Historical Timeline of Israel-Palestine

Diagram: Changes in the Map of Israel 9

Chapter 2 11
The Battle for Land

Chapter 3 19
Injustice: A Temporary State of Existence

Chapter 4 25
Options to Secure Peace

Chapter 5 31
The Five Steps to Peace

Chapter 6 33
The Israeli-Palestinian Peace Proposal

Diagrams

Israel Today 41

Palestine Proposed 42

Two State Solution 43

The West Bank of Palestine Proposed 44

The Gaza Strip of Palestine Proposed 45

Proposed Palestine Mass Transit System 46

Chapter 7 47
Sharing the Land?

Chapter 8 53
The Moshe-Hassan Dialogue

Chapter 9 101
Conclusion

Selected Bibliography 103

Index 105

About The Author 111

"We can live without our friends but not without our neighbors"

—*Thomas Fuller*

Preface

In the spring of 1992, I published an article in the weekly Palestinian newspaper *Al-Fajr,* published in Jerusalem and in Hampstead, New York entitled, "An Israeli-Palestinian Peace Proposal." The article created an uproar within both the Palestinian and Jewish communities, for the proposed compromises were quite controversial, but nevertheless necessary. In fact, the article enraged the readers to such a degree that *Al-Fajr* printed a disclaimer in the following issue stating that the article did not necessarily represent the views of the newspaper. Because it stirred such strong emotion with both peoples, I am convinced this proposal is within reach of a working solution. After all, tensions are highest when negotiating the final details to an agreement; especially in this conflict, where a few key issues are major challenges to be overcome. This proposal is more relevant now than ever, especially in light of the recent Israeli-PLO mutual recognition and autonomy agreements that are just beginning.

On one of my many trips to the Middle East, I came to befriend a senior official in the Israeli Labor Party. Through persistence, I was able to persuade him to participate in a one-on-one conversation with a prominent Palestinian Arab about a potential Israeli-Palestinian peace settlement. Both reluctantly agreed to this two day conversation with the stated condition of anonymity. I refer to the Israeli as *Moshe* and the Palestinian as *Hassan*. The majority of the dialogue itself is included in *Chapter 8* and provides a rare example of two opposing men working out a mutually beneficial solution. The dialogue is the basis for the majority of the *Israeli-Palestinian Peace Proposal* presented in this book.

As neither an Arab nor Jew, I find myself drawn to the conflict in an effort to seek a just solution that will end this tragedy which dominates the Middle East. As an objective outsider, I am able to differentiate between the facts, emotions, and necessary compromises/sacrifices. Those involved are often swayed by emotion and less likely to view the situation objectively. I can only hope that my efforts will have a positive impact on the peace process.

Road To The Holy Land
by Jorge (Mullen) - 1994 oil on canvas

Chapter 1

An Historical Timeline of Israel-Palestine

"History is indeed little more than the register of the crimes, follies, and misfortune of mankind." —Gibbon

Note 1: The lands of present day Israel and the occupied territories of the West Bank and Gaza Strip are referred to as Israel-Palestine.

Note 2: The Israeli-occupied Palestinian land on the western side of the Jordan River is defined as the West Bank.

Timeline

3300 B.C. — Coming from Syria and beyond, the Canaanites migrate and settle in Israel-Palestine. (Palestinians today claim their origin to the Canaanites.)

3000 - 1469 B.C. — Series of invasions and occupations by numerous Semitic tribes.

2000 B.C. — The Jews migrate and settle in Israel-Palestine. After a questionable length of stay, the Jews flee to Egypt because of widespread famine.

1800 B.C. — Time of Biblical Abraham. The Jewish, Muslim, and

Christian faiths all trace their origins to the Patriarch Abraham. God promised the Holy Land of Israel-Palestine to Abraham and his descendants. (Who are the rightful descendants? All three peoples?)

1468 - 1181 B.C. — Egyptian occupation of Israel-Palestine.

1250 B.C. — Exodus of the Jews from Egypt.

1250 - 1200 B.C. — Jewish (Israelite) conquest of Israel-Palestine.

1160 B.C. — The Philistines (Sea Peoples from the Aegean Islands) migrate and settle in the coastal strip of Israel-Palestine. (The Philistines today are an extinct ethnic group, but the Romans later used their name in calling the region Syria-Palestina. 'Palestine' and 'Palestinian' come from this Roman description of the Philistines.)

1160 - 1050 B.C. — Battle for control of Israel-Palestine between the Jews (Israelites) and the Philistines. The Israelite Jews prevail.

1020 - 928 B.C. — United Jewish Kingdom of Israel under Saul, David, and Solomon. Solomon builds the great temple in Jerusalem.

928 B.C. — The Jewish Kingdom divides in two; Israel in the north, Judah in the south.

721 B.C. — Assyrians led by Sargon II conquer and occupy Israel-Palestine.

587 B.C. — Babylonians under Nebuchadnezzar conquer Judah, destroy Jerusalem and the Temple, and annex Israel-Palestine. The Jews are exiled from their lands and enslaved.

539 - 333 B.C. — Persian (Iranian) rule of Israel-Palestine. The Jews are permitted to return and rebuild the Temple.

332 - 312 B.C. — Macedonians led by Alexander the Great conquer and control Israel-Palestine. (Alexander dies prematurely in *323 B.C.*.)

312 - 198 B.C. — Ptolemaic (Egyptian) rule of Israel-Palestine.

198 - 142 B.C. — Seleucid (Persian) conquest and control of Israel-Palestine.

142 - 64 B.C. — Hasmonaean (Maccabaean) rule of Israel-Palestine. (The Jews enjoy both religious and political independence during this period.)

63 B.C. - A.D. 378 — Roman conquest and rule of Israel-Palestine.

A.D. 66 - 73 — Jewish revolt. The Romans burn Jerusalem and destroy the Second Temple. The Jews are either killed, enslaved, or exiled.

A.D. 132 - 135 — Bar Kochba Jewish revolt against Roman rule resulting in the death or expulsion of most Jews in Israel-Palestine.

A.D. 379 - 635 — The Roman Empire divides in two. The eastern half, the Byzantine Empire, takes control of Israel-Palestine.

A.D. 636 - 1098 — Muslim Arab armies conquer and occupy Israel-Palestine.

A.D. 691 — The Muslims erect the gold Dome of the Rock shrine in Jerusalem (on the grounds of the destroyed Jewish Temple). The rock is considered to be the spot of Mohammed's miraculous night journey to heaven. It is the third holiest shrine in Islam, behind Mecca and Medina.

A.D. 710 — The Muslims erect the silver domed Al-Aqsa Mosque in Jerusalem (also on the grounds of the destroyed Jewish Temple).

1095 - 1187 — Christian crusaders from Europe conquer and occupy Israel-Palestine.

1187 - 1204 — Muslim army led by Saladin defeats the crusaders and recaptures Jerusalem.

1204 - 1254 — Christians occupy Israel-Palestine.

1254 - 1292 — Muslims occupy Israel-Palestine.

1292 - 1516 — Mamluks of Egypt rule Israel-Palestine.

1516 - 1918 — Ottoman (Turkish) Empire rules Israel-Palestine.

1882 — First mass immigration of Jews from Russia and Eastern Europe.

1891 — The Arabs of Jerusalem demand that the Ottoman authorities prohibit further Jewish land purchases or immigration to Israel-Palestine.

1896 — Theodore Herzl publishes *The Jewish State*, calling for a Jewish homeland.

1897 — Zionist movement is founded at Basel, Switzerland, at the First Zionist Congress.

1914 - 1918 — World War I.

1916 — The Sykes-Picot Agreement is signed by Britain, France, and Russia to carve up the Ottoman Empire. Britain is to control Israel-Palestine.

1918 — The Ottoman Empire is defeated in World War I and cedes control of Israel-Palestine.

1920 — Britain is given the mandate to control Israel-Palestine and Transjordan under the Palestine Mandate.

1936 - 1939 — Palestinian Arabs revolt against British rule and the theory of a Jewish homeland in Israel-Palestine.

1937 — The British Peel Plan for the partition of Palestine is issued.

1939 — White Paper is issued by the British to limit further Jewish immigration to Israel-Palestine.

1939 -1945 — World War II. Britain is significantly weakened by the war effort.

1945 - 1947 — Influx of Jewish refugees from Europe to Israel-Palestine.

1947 — The United Nations votes to partition Israel-Palestine into two nations—one for the Palestinian Arabs and one for the Jews. Jerusalem will be maintained as an international city.

1948 — Israel declares independence. Six Arab armies attack to prevent the creation of Israel. The Israelis decisively defeat the Arab armies and gain more land than the U.N. plan called for (including West Jerusalem). Israel is established, but a homeland for the Palestinian Arabs ceases to exist. Jordan occupies the West Bank/East Jerusalem and Egypt occupies the Gaza Strip. Approximately nine-hundred thousand Palestinian Arabs flee as refugees during the war.

1956 — Israel, Britain, and France attack Egypt and occupy the Sinai in an effort to secure the Suez Canal from Nasser's threats to close the Suez Canal to international shipping. Israel withdraws under pressure from the United States and the Soviet Union.

1964 — The Palestine Liberation Organization (PLO) is established by the Arab League to act as an umbrella organization for the eight Palestine liberation groups. The PLO charter calls for the destruction of the Zionist state of Israel.

1967 — Six Day War. Israel launches a preemptive military strike against Egypt, Syria, and Jordan with great success. Israel conquers and occupies the Sinai, Gaza Strip, Golan Heights, East Jerusalem, and all of the West Bank. Approximately four-hundred and ten thousand additional Palestinian Arabs become war refugees. Israel quickly annexes East Jerusalem and proclaims Jerusalem as its unified capital.

1967 November 22 — United Nations Security Council Resolution 242 is passed calling for the withdrawal of all Israeli forces from the occupied territories and for Arab recognition of the State of Israel.

1969 — Yasir Arafat (of Al-Fatah) is elected chairman of the PLO.

1970 — King Hussein defeats and ousts the PLO in a bloody civil war for control of Jordan. The PLO withdraws and relocates to Lebanon.

1972-1988 — The PLO and other Palestinian terrorist organizations wage a war of international terrorism against Israeli and

American interests. Although a policy of brutality, it was very successful at publicizing the Palestinian cause.

1973 — Yom Kippur War - Egypt and Syria stage a surprise attack against Israel with initial success. Israel, with the aid of an American airlift of supplies, eventually defeats the Arab armies.

1973 October 22 — United Nations Security Council Resolution 338 is passed calling for the implementation of Resolution 242 and a peaceful settlement to the Palestinian problem.

1974 — The Arab Summit in Morocco claims the PLO as the "sole and legitimate representative" of the Palestinian people.

1974 — The United Nations recognizes the PLO as the representative of the Palestinian people.

1975 November 10 — The United Nations General Assembly passes a resolution describing Zionism as a "form of racism and racial discrimination."

1977 — Egyptian President Anwar Sadat visits Jerusalem offering peace in exchange for an Israeli withdrawal from Sinai.

1979 — Israeli Prime Minister Menachem Begin and Egyptian President Anwar Sadat sign a peace treaty. Israel agrees to a complete withdrawal from the Sinai Peninsula.

1981 — Egyptian President Anwar Sadat is assassinated by Muslim extremists.

1981 December — Israel annexes the Golan Heights that it conquered from Syria in the 1967 war.

1982 — Israel invades Lebanon to expel the PLO. (An Israeli version of the U.S. experience in Vietnam.)

1982 August — Yasir Arafat and the PLO withdraw from Lebanon and relocate to Tunis, Tunisia.

1985 — Israel withdraws from Lebanon, but maintains a security zone in southern Lebanon.

1987 December — The Palestinian Intifada (uprising) spreads throughout the occupied territories.

1988 November — Yasir Arafat and the Palestine National Congress (PNC) declare an independent Palestinian state, but with undefined borders.

1988 December 13 — Yasir Arafat and the PLO vaguely recognize Israel's right to exist and renounce all forms of terrorism. The United States opens dialogue with the PLO.

1990 Spring — The United States cuts off dialogue with the PLO for Arafat's refusal to renounce a failed terrorist attack on Israel and his refusal to dismiss the man responsible, Abul Abbas, from the executive committee of the Palestine National Congress (PNC).

1990 August — Iraq invades Kuwait. Yasir Arafat, the PLO, and the vast majority of Palestinian people, against world opinion, support Saddam Hussein.

1990 Fall — Saudi Arabia and many of the Persian Gulf Kingdoms cut off financial support to the PLO for its support of Iraq.

1991 January — Persian Gulf War. Iraq is easily defeated, but succeeds in hitting Israel with a series of Scud Missiles.

1991 — Kuwaiti war crimes trials and persecution of Palestinians for their support of Saddam Hussein.

1991 July — Syrian President Hafez Al Assad agrees to direct talks with Israel.

1991 - 1993 — The ongoing Arab-Israeli and Palestinian Arab-Israeli peace negotiations proceed with little substantive progress.

1993 — The United Nations General Assembly repeals its 1975 resolution equating Zionism with a "form of racism and racial discrimination."

1993 July — Israel attacks radical Arab positions in Lebanon in the largest scale fighting since the 1982 invasion.

August-September 1993 — Israel admits to high level secret negotiations with the PLO and recognizes the PLO as the legitimate representative of the Palestinian people. The PLO, in turn, recognizes the right of the State of Israel to exist in peace and security. Furthermore, the PLO renounces the use of terrorism and other acts of violence.

September 1993 — The United States reopens dialogue with the PLO.

September 1993 — The Gaza-Jericho First Autonomy Plan is announced as the first step toward Palestinian autonomy in the occupied territories. Negotiations on a final settlement are to begin in two to three years.

September - February 1994 — The negotiations aimed at implementing the Gaza-Jericho First Autonomy Plan stall over several key border issues.

February 1994 — Baruch Goldstein, a Jewish settler, massacres twenty-nine Palestinian worshippers in the Tomb of the Patriarchs in Hebron. In protest, the P.L.O., Jordan, Syria and Lebanon refuse to continue negotiating with Israel until measures are taken to protect Palestinians in the occupied territories.

March 1994 — The peace negotiations resume after Israel makes concessions to the Palestinians.

May 1994 — Israeli Prime Minister Yitzhak Rabin and PLO leader Yasir Arafat sign and begin implementing the delayed Gaza-Jericho First Autonomy Plan authorizing limited Palestinian autonomy in the Gaza Strip and the West Bank town of Jericho.

July 1994 — Israeli Prime Minister Yitzhak Rabin and King Hussein of Jordan publicly terminate the 'state of war' between their nations and begin working on the details to a formal peace treaty.

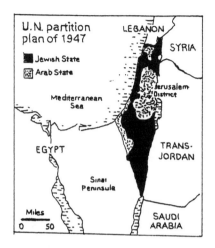

Changes in the Map of Israel

Chapter 2

The Battle For Land

"The equal right of all men to the use of land is as clear as their equal right to breathe the air — it is a right proclaimed by the fact of their existence. For we cannot suppose that some men have a right to be in this world, and others no right."
—Henry George

Since the creation of the modern state of Israel in 1948, we have witnessed the ongoing Arab-Israeli conflict and its negative impact on the Middle East and the world community. The conflict has created general misery through the widespread use of warfare, terrorism, and the ballooning refugee situation. For the first time since 1979, real progress is being made toward an Arab-Israeli peace settlement, but first a comprehensive Israeli-Palestinian Arab peace settlement must be established before most of the Arab nations will venture toward formal peace with Israel. Egyptian President Anwar Sadat made peace with Israel in 1979 and was subsequently assassinated in 1981 for this action. The Arab peoples are emotionally attached to the plight of the Palestinians under Israeli occupation and will resist peace settlements until the Palestinian question is justly satisfied. Once a just Israeli-Palestinian peace proposal is achieved, the opportunity will be available for a general Arab-Israeli peace settlement not yet seen. Jordan's King Hussein has long wanted a peace agreement with Israel, but the political realities of the Middle East have prevented him from doing so. Syria also is prepared for peace with Israel if territorial concessions on the Golan Heights can be agreed upon. This may be their opportunity, for Israel is finally at the negotiating table. Further peace treaties would almost be assured with Morocco, Saudi Arabia, and the Gulf Kingdoms. Even Syrian dominated Lebanon would be more willing to negotiate. Iran, Iraq, and Libya would resist and be unlikely to extend overtures of peace under any conditions short of an Israeli withdrawal to Brooklyn, New York.

It is important to note that the recent Israeli-PLO mutual recognition agreement and the plan for partial Palestinian autonomy under the Gaza-Jericho First Plan are developments in the right direction, but they are only the beginning. Negotiations on a final Palestinian settlement are not even scheduled to begin for two to three years. When they do occur, there is no guarantee that a peace settlement will be reached. We must remember that Israel has long wanted to relinquish its control over the troublesome Gaza Strip, but neither Egypt nor Jordan has been interested in acquiring it. The agreement with the PLO may have been the only viable option for Israel to rid itself of the Gaza Strip. Whether this plan is the first of many steps or a one time occurrence out of Israeli necessity remains to be seen. The controversial issues have yet to be addressed.

Furthermore, the Israeli-PLO agreements have an excellent chance of spurring an Israeli peace settlement with Jordan and/or Syria. Although this would be a positive development, it would also be quite premature because the Israeli-Palestinian conflict is far from settled. If the Israeli-Palestinian peace process were to unravel without a comprehensive Palestinian settlement, it could unleash a violent backlash within both the occupied territories and those Arab states that rushed to make peace with Israel. The situation would be especially precarious in Jordan where the population itself is over seventy percent Palestinian. Now that the peace process is finally moving forward, prudence and caution are recommended for both peoples. Agreements entered in haste generally are not solid foundations for long-term success.

In the Western world, the nature of the Israeli-Palestinian conflict is generally misunderstood and misdiagnosed in two fashions:
1. As an historical conflict dating to Biblical times, and
2. As a religiously based conflict of hate.
Both of these explanations are wrong and serve only to rationalize the existence of the conflict, but do little to define it. Historically speaking, the Muslim Arabs have treated the Jews far better than the Christian European powers have. Examples of this are the Spanish Inquisition, the French crackdowns, the pogroms in Russia-Poland, and the Nazi German holocaust. There is no historically based hate between Islam and Judaism, but there is with Christianity. This is the result of the Jewish sanction of Jesus Christ's crucifixion. Even with this historical conflict, Israel today is closely allied with most of the Christian European powers that previously tormented their Jewish communities. In addition, the European Christian powers have had major historical conflicts with the Muslim Arabs dating to the fall of the Byzantine Empire and the Holy Crusades of the Middle Ages. The Muslim-Christian tension is still evident today.

Both the Jews and Muslim Arabs are Semitic peoples whose religions spawn from the Patriarch Abraham. Neither religion mandates the killing of the other. Prior to the twentieth century, there have been endless examples of Jews and Muslim Arabs living side by side harmoniously. Unfortunately, the radical factions describe this current conflict as a religious 'holy war' to the death to serve their own purposes. The Jewish extremists (e.g., Temple Mount Faithful, Kach) and the Palestinian extremists (e.g., Hamas, Islamic Jihad) are the only beneficiaries to this religious rationalization of war. In reality, it is a recent conflict created in the twentieth century—a conflict based on the battle for the lands of Israel-Palestine.

Historians have identified over twenty-seven distinct occupations of Israel-Palestine. (See *Chapter 1* for the historical outline). This geographical area has been conquered and reconquered since before the time of Biblical Abraham. Today the Jews are in control, but tomorrow it may be the Syrians, Iranians (Persians), or Turks. The Jews have been displaced before and that risk is always pending.

From 1516 to 1918, the lands of Israel-Palestine were under Ottoman (Turkish) rule. Jews and Palestinian Arabs lived side by side and had both working and personal relationships. Due to the 1882 pogroms in Russia and Poland, Jewish immigration to Israel-Palestine increased dramatically. A Palestinian xenophobic response developed against the influx of European Jewish immigrants and their ideals of a Jewish homeland. This was not a surprising reaction since the Zionist homeland was to be built on the lands of Palestinian Arabs. Whether justifiable or not, the Palestinians feared for the future of their land and community. The following fifty years became a battle for land. In 1948, the Jews became the victors, the Palestinians the vanquished. In the Six Day War of 1967, Israel expanded that victory to include the occupied territories of the West Bank, Gaza Strip, Golan Heights, Sinai Peninsula, and East Jerusalem.

Palestinian Arabs who lost the 1890-1948 and 1967 battles for the land are openly contesting the outcome. The displaced Palestinians want their land, or a portion of it, returned to them. The surrounding Arab states sympathize with this because the Palestinian people are of the same ethnic background and religion. Moreover, most of the Arab states have suffered humiliating defeats to the Israelis and do not relish those memories.

Today, the Palestinians argue that the land they lived on for centuries was taken from them by immigrating European Jews. The Jews claim their legitimacy to the land by the fact that they owned this land two thousand years ago before the expulsion by the Romans. Both claim ancestral links and rights to the land dating back to the time of Biblical Abraham three thousand eight hundred years ago. There is no clear historical proof of either peoples' sole right to the land. It is a land of historical conquest and resultant displaced peoples. We cannot attempt to correct this history of misery. Instead, we must work on the situation as it stands today with the goal of making the current situation better.

The English and French were at war for half a millennium and yet today they are close allies. Few would have imagined this possibility in the sixteenth through nineteenth centuries. Similarly, the Israeli-Palestinian conflict can be solved given the proper medicine. This conflict is quite young (since the 1890's) in comparison to the English-French standoff. Western principles support the rights of self-determination for all peoples. Therefore, both the Jews and Palestinians have the legal right to create their own nation and destiny. But what if both peoples want to create their nation and destiny in the same land? Are they destined to perpetual conflict as we have witnessed in the twentieth century? Not in this situation, because the people are now separated into distinct geographic areas. The areas are quite small, but separate nevertheless. The Jews are primarily in Israel proper and the Palestinians in the Gaza Strip and West Bank. The issue of Jewish settlers in the occupied territories is a serious one, but cannot be allowed to act as an impediment to a general peace settlement. The Jews have fulfilled their right to self-determination, but the Palestinians have not been allowed the same opportunity. Under the principles of justice and fair play, the Palestinians must be allowed to form a homeland as long as it does not jeopardize or call upon the destruction of Israel.

The creation of a Palestinian state is the only just solution available that will defuse the Israeli-Palestinian and the Israeli-Arab conflicts. However, this state must be in accordance with the security concerns of Israel. In addition, the Palestinians must see their statehood as a solution to the conflict that they can have respect for and take pride in.

Since 1948, the peace process has been virtually non-existent, with the notable exception of the Israeli-Egyptian peace treaty of 1979. Other vague references to peace have been made, but very little time has been spent focusing on how a detailed peace plan can be achieved. The Fahd Plan (1982) issued by Saudi Crown Prince Fahd is unacceptable to Israel for it reiterates most of the PLO demands, such as Israel's return to its pre-1967 borders, the establishment of a Palestinian state with East Jerusalem as its capital, and the dismantling of all Jewish settlements in now-occupied territory. Similarly, the Reagan Plan (1982) is a one-sided proposal in favor of Israel, but does little for the Palestinians, since it rejects the principle of an independent Palestinian state, but instead proposes Palestinian autonomy and calls for a temporary freeze on building Jewish settlements in occupied territories but not for dismantling them. One may wonder why either plan was put forward. Neither proposes any genuine compromises worth consideration.

In May 1988, Jerome M. Segal, a research scholar at the Institute of Philosophy and Public Policy at the University of Maryland, College Park, issued a strategy for the PLO to declare an independent state of Palestine in the territories without Israeli approval. The PLO followed Segal's advice and subsequently issued a Palestinian declaration of independence (with its capital as Jerusalem) on November 15, 1988, but to no avail. Israel's military superiority and sophisticated network of Palestinian informers then and now cripple any Palestinian attempts at statehood. The only solution is to gain Israeli approval and that is not going to be easy. Substantial compromises are necessary for the Palestinians to get Israeli acceptance of statehood and this will include an unpopular sacrifice on the highly controversial issue of Jerusalem.

Until recently, the Israelis have declined to comment on the details of a peace settlement, for they have had little intention of making the necessary compromises. The Palestinians have issued vague references to accepting a partial homeland or a confederation with Jordan, but they also have not discussed a realistic plan with detail. They understandably hesitate for fear of making sacrifices to deaf Israeli ears. (One loses respect by making sacrifices to an adversary that is not negotiating. The PLO learned this lesson in 1988 in recognizing Israel's right to exist for which Israel failed to respond.)

The current peace dialogue initiated by U.S. President George Bush in 1991 had produced little progress until the Gaza-Jericho First Autonomy Proposal of September 1993. The impact of this proposal remains to be seen. Dialogue is generally considered a positive development, but in this conflict, it may do more harm than good if no substantive results are put forth. Dialogue is important, but only if both sides have genuine compromises to offer. We can only hope that Gaza-Jericho First is the beginning of a dialogue based on compromise. The most significant break-through has been the Israeli recognition of the PLO and the PLO recognition of Israel. For the first time, the leaders of both peoples can openly negotiate with each other.

A systematic blueprint outlining a peace settlement is vital to the continuation of the peace process, yet neither side has put one forward. The mutual recognition agreement and the Gaza-Jericho First Autonomy Plan are steps in the right direction, but are not a final settlement or a blueprint for a final settlement. How can one create a successful peace settlement without a blueprint for building it? Vague references of Palestinian autonomy or an independent Palestinian state in the territories are not sufficient. Demands from Washington D.C., PLO headquarters, or Jerusalem are not blueprints. What we need is a highly detailed outline of what could succeed in developing an Israeli-Palestinian settlement. With that blueprint, both sides can haggle on the particulars and, it is hoped, hammer out an agreement that will work for both communities.

This book is dedicated to implementing an acceptable Israeli-Palestinian settlement that will lead to a general atmosphere of peace in the Middle East. The peace proposal put forth in *Chapter 6* is a concise 'blueprint' for an Israeli-Palestinian settlement that addresses the issues of both peoples. It contains genuine compromises by both sides. It is not perfect, but it is a platform upon which both sides can negotiate. Neither side is exclusively to blame for the conflict. Both bear guilt and innocence in this tragic situation. My goal is not to take sides, but solely to seek a solution that is both viable and acceptable.

The responsibility of action lies with the Israelis and Palestinians. No one can do it for them. Not the United Nations, not the European community, and not even the United States can solve this puzzle. When these two troublesome brothers, Israel and Palestine, come to see that their future is dependent upon the other's success, then and only then will they move forward to achieving peace. The recent mutual recognition by Israel and the PLO is a signal that both communities are coming to this realization.

The Search For Justice
by Jorge (Mullen) - 1993 oil on canvas

Chapter 3

Injustice: A Temporary State of Existence

"Wherever there is a human being, I see God-given rights inherent in that being, whatever may be the sex or complexion."
—William Lloyd Garrison

"He who commits injustice is ever made more wretched than he who suffers it." —Plato

The Mullen Theory of Injustice: Governments or individuals which govern through policies of injustice by restricting the inherent rights of all or part of their peoples are destined to premature failure. Inherent rights are defined as those which Western democracies view as God-given: Life, liberty, the pursuit of happiness, self-determination, and equality.

When a government or individual strives to restrict the inherent rights of another, there exists the state of injustice. Injustice is a temporary state of existence that people will risk their lives to replace with justice. Furthermore, governments built on policies of injustice are doomed to premature failure. The unjust governments of Nazi Germany, East Germany, the Soviet Union, and Apartheid South Africa were all doomed to failure from the onset. Some last longer than others, but all ultimately crumble due to a lack of moral standing.

History has repeatedly proven to us that governments based on policies of injustice have very limited futures. Those subjected to injustice eventually strike back when the opportunity arises, often leading to civil war or revolution. Examples of this are the United States (1776 and 1861), France (1789), Russia (1917), and Iran (1979). It is important to note that the government which follows a civil war is not always for the better. (e.g., Russia, Iran).

The governmental systems that prevail protect the peoples' inherent rights and provide them with the belief that their system is equally just to all. Prime examples are the United States, Great Britain, France, and Canada. Governments based on justice are nearly impossible to undermine from within. Citizens treated fairly are not motivated to risk their lives by overturning a system that has protected their rights. This is not to say that the democracies of the United States and Great Britain are perfect, but they are successful. Both systems are based on fair principles of equality and provide their citizens with paths of recourse against government abuse and unfair treatment.

Both the Israelis and Palestinians are guilty of practicing policies of injustice against the other. The atmosphere created by these policies will lead to an armed conflict if they are allowed to continue.

Israel is a dualist society that does not treat all of the people equally or fairly. It is a progressive democratic society based on just policies for its Jewish citizens. The two million Palestinians under Israeli occupation, on the other hand, are treated with disdain and contempt. They are not treated with the same equality or justice that the Jewish citizens enjoy. The Palestinians are held under military martial law and are not given the opportunity to fulfill their inherent rights of liberty, pursuit of happiness, self-determination or equality. They are viewed as second-class citizens that do not deserve the same inherent rights as the Jewish citizens. This is akin to the United States' former practice of slavery, apartheid in South Africa and British India, all of which practiced dualist policies with first and second tier citizenry. The dualist approach is an unjust discriminatory policy based on the false rationalization that an entire segment of society should be held down for the good of the state. When in fact, this approach leads to the decay of the state from within. The United States, South Africa, and British India all experienced tremendous violence to overturn their unjust dualist policies. In Israel, this dualist policy is degrading to the high quality democratic government.

The Israelis rationalize their policies, with noteworthy justification, by claiming they preserve the national security. In essence, Israel will do what is necessary to protect herself. If that includes denying a segment of society its inherent rights, so be it. Israel is a democracy, and democracies are not prone to supporting aggressive actions or unwarranted practices; therefore, they must have concrete reasoning for their policies. The terrorist onslaught directed at Israel merits these policies, unjust as some may be.

There is however, no merit or justice to the Israeli policy of settling over one-hundred and thirty thousand of its citizens in the occupied territories. In essence, the first class citizens (Israeli) are being given land stolen from the second class citizens (Palestinian). Was the Nazi policy of confiscating homes of German Jews and giving them to Nazi party members a just policy? Was Nazi Germany's policy of settlement in occupied Poland and Western Russia a just policy? Absolutely not, and neither is Israel's policy just. The attempt to legitimize this act is repulsive to all who believe in International Law. Historical justification dating to Biblical times is not sufficient basis for taking another's land. The act of one's ancestor does not empower a distant descendant to steal land back. Occupied territories should not be forcibly settled. Those Israelis who wish to settle in the territories should be required to have approval from those who rightfully own the land. Israeli security may be a reasonable justification for holding the occupied territories, but not for building settlements on it.

The threat of armed civil war by the nearly two million Palestinians in the occupied territories is a very real possibility if the Palestinians continue to be treated unjustly. The desperation level is high and it is widely known that the Palestinians have been stockpiling weapons and ammunition for decades. One day, they will resort to the widespread use of these weapons if they are not allowed to fulfill their inherent rights.

The Palestinians, likewise, have practiced organized policies of injustice against Israel. The Palestine Liberation Organization (PLO), as the representative body of the Palestinians, has

1. denied Israel the right to exist,
2. denied Israeli citizens the right to live in safe, definable borders, and
3. even denied many Israeli citizens the right to live.

The Palestinian Intifada (Uprising) has sanctioned the stabbing of Israeli citizens and soldiers, which has served only to heighten tensions between these communities. By sponsoring organized terrorism and anti-Israeli rhetoric, the Palestinians have clearly pursued polices of injustice bent on harming Israel. The Palestinians justify their policies as being their only recourse in their fight for freedom and their inherent rights. In their eyes, they are a desperate people, backed into a corner, with nothing left to lose. And in this argument there is also merit, for no one seems to hear the Palestinians unless they resort to violence.

There are many hardline Israelis that would welcome the opportunity to kill and/or permanently exile a majority of the Palestinian community. The Palestinian policies are quite risky, for they could give the extremist Israeli leaders the justification and support for armed action. Israel is the military superpower of the Middle East and, if sufficiently provoked, she will strike with the Sword of Gideon at those threatening her.

The policies of injustice by both the Israelis and Palestinians have created a vicious cycle of violence and hate. The cycle goes as follows: The Palestinians sponsor terrorist activity to combat the Israeli occupation of the territories. The subsequent terrorist activity prompts Israel, for security purposes, to deny the Palestinians their inherent rights. In turn, the Palestinians increase the heat with both rhetoric and violent attacks against Israeli citizens. Israel responds with house demolitions and military curfews. The cycle continues and escalates at each new stage, and if it ever gets out of control, the result will be armed combat and massacres. No one wins.

Both the Israeli and Palestinian governments are destined to premature failure because of their unjust policies. However, the Palestinians do not have a state to lose. The policies of injustice have put the future of the state of Israel in question. The Palestinians will someday strike back and with the aid of the surrounding Arab states, may possibly win. The wrath of a suppressed Palestinian minority suddenly put in power is not an event Israeli citizens want to experience. The United States and Great Britain may not always be there to resupply or rescue an embattled Israel.

Israel must take the initiative on this issue, but the Palestinians must follow suit quickly. Both peoples must begin pursuing policies of justice toward the other. The Palestinians will have to honor Israel's right to exist in safe, definable borders, just as the Israelis will have to honor the equality of the Palestinians and their right to self-determination. The Israelis will view this as a great security risk, but it will not be as risky as maintaining the *status quo* of injustice.

The Israeli-PLO mutual recognition agreement is the first step toward justice for both peoples. When these words of justice are backed up by actions of justice, there will exist a legitimate society and state.

Chapter 4

Options to Secure Peace

"Revolutions are not made; they come." —Wendell Phillips

Israel has five principal options in dealing with the Palestinian problem in the occupied territories:

1. *Maintain the status quo of occupation* — This is an unacceptable position for it does not deal with the festering problem, and it denies the Palestinians their inherent rights. Israel would not be able to control the territories indefinitely with their current policies. The risk of a civil war against the Israeli authorities would increase with time.

2. *Exile the entire Palestinian community to Jordan and Lebanon* — This is an open violation of International Law and the Fourth Geneva Convention to which Israel is a signatory. It would backfire on Israel and result in a dramatic increase in the security risk on all borders. This policy should never be entertained, for the State of Israel would lose all foundation of legitimacy.

3. *Establish Palestinian autonomy under Israeli auspices* — This option may succeed in the short run, but would not placate the Palestinian desires for self-determination. There would continue to be some type of Israeli presence which the Palestinians would resent and work to undermine. Eventually, Israel would reoccupy the territories for security purposes, justifiably so or not.

Limited autonomy for Gaza-Jericho or full autonomy for all the occupied territories will not end the conflict. The Gaza-Jericho First Autonomy proposal is an historic breakthrough, but it is only the beginning. It does not address the controversial issues of Palestinian statehood, the West Bank, Jerusalem, the Jewish settlements in the territories, or the Israeli military presence in the territories. The autonomy plan must be used as the first step toward a more substantive settlement that resolves all of these issues.

Moreover, Gaza-Jericho First is a divisive approach that could pit Palestinians against each other if the West Bank is not quickly included. Granting autonomy to the quiet desert city of Jericho and the overpopulated tumultuous Gaza Strip is asking for trouble. (Jericho has a population of fifteen thousand while the Gaza Strip has over eight-hundred and fifty thousand.) There exists a strong Palestinian national cohesiveness that must be cultivated for peace to prevail. The division of the West Bank and Gaza Strip could destroy that cohesiveness by creating a competitive environment where people feel betrayed and abandoned. If the national cohesiveness is lost, the Palestinians will spin out of control with violence, terrorist activity, Islamic Fundamentalism, and a loss of moral dignity. For this reason, the entire West Bank, with its population of nine-hundred and twenty thousand, is needed in the Autonomy Proposal to act as a balance to the Gaza Strip. Without the West Bank, Gaza will consume Jericho into its turbulent problems. The risk would be great to both the State of Israel and the Palestinian community.

4. *Establish a Palestinian confederation with Jordan* — In this scenario an external power (Jordan) would once again be in control of the Palestinian people in the occupied territories. The Palestinian right to self-determination would continue to be denied, for less than forty percent of Palestinians in the territories support confederation even as a secondary solution. Confederation should only be sought if it becomes the democratic choice of both the Palestinian and Jordanian people. The West Bank and East Jerusalem were ruled by Jordan from 1948-1967, and in 1988 King Hussein officially ceased all claims and territorial ties

to the region. Moreover, Jordan does not have any interest in an arrangement with the burdensome Gaza Strip.

Although Jordan itself has a Palestinian majority (seventy percent), it remains under rule of the Jordanian Hashemite monarchy. Jordan's King Hussein is an asset to both the international community and the Middle East. A confederation would serve to destabilize King Hussein and the region itself. Jordan has had major problems with the Palestinians and the PLO before, in 1970, and should not risk a repeat. A new Jordanian-Palestinian power struggle would not be suitable to peaceful coexistence with Israel. In addition, the prospect of an Iraqi-Jordanian unification would put the outskirts of Jerusalem in Baghdad's reach. The Jordanian and Iraqi peoples share many of the same interests and the possibility of unification cannot be ruled out. It is in both the interests of Israel and the world community to preserve King Hussein's position as it is.

5. *Adoption of a two-state solution through the creation of Palestine alongside Israel* — This is the only viable option that promotes justice, security and peace for the region. Nearly 100 percent of the Palestinian populace supports the creation of a State of Palestine. Their majority, along with suitable security arrangements, will bring about peaceful coexistence. The cultivation of the Palestinian national cohesiveness will prompt the Palestinians to shift their focus away from subverting Israel toward building Palestine.

The two-state solution, however, presents tremendous risks to both the Israelis and Palestinians. The Israelis are in the dominant position and therefore must seek a solution with the greatest likelihood of long-term success. The risks can be minimized by strict supervision and monitoring of the situation and Israel will always have the back door escape of reoccupation if the situation turned for the worse.

People Without A Homeland
by Jorge (Mullen) - 1993 oil on canvas

Chapter 5

The Five Steps to Peace

"All government—indeed, every human benefit and enjoyment, every virtue and every prudent act—is founded on compromise and barter." —Edmund Burke

In order to reach a successful Israeli-Palestinian settlement, we must initiate a strategy aimed at finding a common ground between both peoples. With this agreed upon, the Israeli and Palestinian diplomats will have the opportunity to craft a mutually acceptable settlement. Without it, the negotiations will end in an argumentative stalemate as we have repeatedly seen. Five central premises, which I refer to as the "Five Steps to Peace," outline the common ground necessary for the peace process to move forward.

First and foremost, the Israeli and Palestinian populace must accept the fact that compromise is a necessity in addressing each other's interests and achieving peace. Lasting peace can only succeed with give and take by both peoples.

Second, the history of Israel-Palestine and its people must be detached from the peace process. Negotiations should be based on the conditions as they stand today.

Dredging up the tragic history in an attempt to correct its injustices will only serve to aggravate the current situation.

Third, the Israelis need to honor the Palestinian people's right for self-determination. The overwhelming consensus of the Palestinian populace mandates their right to statehood. A separate state, however small, will provide the Palestinians with what they need—pride, independence, and a homeland to build—and the focus will shift from subverting Israel to building Palestine. Palestinians routinely disagree on the politics of an independent state, but I have yet to meet one Palestinian that does not crave an independent Palestine.

Fourth, the Palestinians must agree to an independent state that does not include Jerusalem or the other areas of concern to Israeli security. Moreover, the Palestinians must recognize Jerusalem as the capital and sole property of Israel. Though a sore point to all Palestinians, this is a necessity, for Israel will never tolerate a Palestinian state that puts Jerusalem in jeopardy. By relinquishing their territorial claim to the city, the Palestinians will allay Israeli fears and open the door to statehood for the West Bank and Gaza. In exchange, Palestinian interests in Jerusalem, such as concessions for worship, commerce, and tourism will receive recognition by the Israelis. Furthermore, the Palestinians residing in Jerusalem today will maintain all of their interests in Jerusalem as equal Israeli citizens under the full protection of Israeli law. Palestinian ownership of homes, land, businesses, and holy sites in Jerusalem are all examples of these interests.

Fifth, a comprehensive and detailed blueprint for peace must be created based on the common ground of both peoples.

The mutual acceptance of the "Five Steps to Peace" will lead to genuine negotiations and a lasting peace not yet seen in Israel-Palestine. It will mark the beginning of a new era in Middle Eastern diplomacy.

Peace With Hands, No More Fighting With Arms
Destroyed Egyptian artillery in the Negev Desert
Photo: Mullen (1986)

Chapter 6

The Israeli-Palestinian Peace Proposal

"Peace be within thy walls, and prosperity within thy palaces."
—Psalms CXX11.7

Peace Proposal - Outline

I. The creation of an independent Palestinian state in modified borders of the occupied territories is the only option available that will establish the basis for a lasting Israeli-Palestinian peace. A series of conditions will be agreed upon to satisfy Israeli security concerns and to ensure the success and safety of the State of Palestine.

II. The State of Palestine will encompass the majority of the West Bank and Gaza with the following exceptions:
   A. Jerusalem and the surrounding designated areas.
   B. Latrun and the adjacent territory reaching to the outskirts of Ramallah and Qalqiliya.
   C. The section north of Jenin and bordering the Jordan River.
   D. Southern region along the border and south of Hebron
   E. The northernmost part of the Gaza.
   (See attached maps)

that of Israel.

    A. The capital will be Hebron.

    B. The population will be two to five million people depending on the number of refugees who return.

    C. Palestine will have access to the Jordan River, Mediterranean Sea, and the Dead Sea.

    D. International borders will be shared with Israel, Jordan, and Egypt.

    E. A highway/railroad corridor will be built from the West Bank area of Hebron to Gaza.

    F. Palestine will maintain two international airports.

       1. Airports will be located along the Dead Sea and on the coast of Gaza.

       2. A joint Israeli-Palestinian commission will be established to route commercial flight paths.

    G. A large harbor facility will be built in Gaza.

    H. Railroad/mass transit system will be built connecting all of Palestine.

IV. Palestine will cede all territorial rights to Jerusalem, while the Palestinian people maintain their historical ties to the Holy City.

    A. Citizens of Palestine will be granted easy access to East Jerusalem and all the holy sites.

    B. Palestine will honor Jerusalem as the capital and sole property of Israel.

    C. Israel will honor the Palestinian religious, family, and commercial interests in Jerusalem.

    D. East Jerusalem Palestinians will maintain full citizenship and equal protection under Israeli law.

    E. East Jerusalem Palestinians will be permitted to carry joint citizenship.

    F. Citizens of Palestine will be allowed to work in East Jerusalem without Israeli citizenship or work visas.

    G. Jerusalem will never be represented in the government of Palestine.

    H. Palestinians from Jerusalem or Israel proper will be

H. Palestinians from Jerusalem or Israel proper will be forbidden to hold political office in Palestine.
I. Palestine will not tax the East Jerusalem Palestinians.
J. The Muslim holy sites of Jerusalem (e.g., The Dome of the Rock, Al Aqsa Mosque) will continue to be administered and protected by the Islamic Waqf (Trust).
K. A commission of three Jews, three Muslims, and three Christians will be formed to oversee the protection of religious freedom in Jerusalem.
L. Freedom of religious practice will be protected under Israeli law.
M. All holy sites in Jerusalem will remain open to both the public and tourists.

V. The transitional government of Palestine will be formed under Israeli occupation.

A. General Palestinian elections will be held six months from today to elect a transitional government consisting of a president, vice president, and a one hundred-member Congress.
  1. The election will be democratic.
  2. United Nations advisors will monitor the election for fairness.
B. All Palestinians will be permitted to vote, with the exception of:
  1. Jailed or detained Palestinians.
  2. Palestinians from the diaspora, those who reside outside Israel and the occupied territories.
  3. Palestinians from Jerusalem or Israel.
C. The transitional government will last four years with the responsibility of establishing a constitution, a bill of rights, a judiciary, laws, peace treaties, and so forth.
D. Palestine will be a democratic state modeled on that of the United States.
E. Elections will occur every four years for President, Vice President, and Congress, with a limit of two successive terms for each.

F. Six months after the transitional government is established, the Israeli Civil Administration will begin the transfer of civil affairs to the new government.
   1. Month 7 - Schools and University administration.
   2. Month 8 - Public works and repair.
   3. Month 9 - Water, electricity and sewage.
   4. Month 10 - Food distribution and mail service.
   5. Month 11 - Hospitals, health care and welfare.
   6. Month 12 - Transportation systems.
   7. Month 13 - Police, fire and other emergency units.
G. All Israeli settlers in the territories will be removed by the IDF (Israeli Defense Forces) and the settlement housing will be preserved for Palestinian use.
H. The Israeli occupation will end after month twenty-four of the existence of the transitional government.
I. After the Israeli withdrawal, Palestine will take control of immigration/border affairs and all other responsibilities.

VI. A formal peace treaty between Israel and Palestine will be signed and ratified by both governments. Terms include:
   A. Both states agree to affirm the border arrangements.
      1. Palestine will recognize Israel's borders, including Jerusalem and the annexed areas of the occupied territories.
      2. Israel will honor the new borders of Palestine.
   B. Israel and Palestine will never attempt to redraw the borders or occupy the other.
   C. Palestine will remain neutral in Middle Eastern affairs and act as the Switzerland of the Middle East.
   D. A mutual defense pact will be enacted that contains a commitment to aid the other in the event of attack.
   E. Terrorism and all terrorist organizations will be denounced and outlawed.
   F. A formal renouncement will be signed that negates all claims the state or individuals hold on the other regarding property or financial compensation.

G. Palestine will be the sole representative of the Palestinian people.

H. Israel agrees to recognize the Palestinian religious and ancestral links to East Jerusalem.

I. Israel will maintain an easy access policy to Jerusalem for all citizens of Palestine.

J. A mutual agreement for the freedom of religious practice in Jerusalem will be signed into law.

K. Both states will endorse a policy promoting tourist and commercial exchange.

L. Both states will establish mandatory secondary school educational programs on the history of the Israeli-Palestinian conflict and the subsequent peace arrangements.

VII. Security arrangements in the Israel-Palestine peace treaty include:

A. Palestine will not maintain offensive forces or weaponry, but a strictly defensive capability.

B. No foreign armed forces, except that of the United Nations, will be permitted access to Palestine.

C. No foreign airforce or navy will be permitted to enter Palestinian air or water space.

D. No nuclear, atomic, chemical, or biological weapons are ever to enter or be developed in Palestine.

E. Palestine will patrol all borders systematically to deter terrorist activity against Israel.

F. The Hebron-Gaza corridor will be fenced, mined and patrolled. Terrorist infiltration from the corridor may result in its closure.

G. A three kilometer dead zone will be maintained along all the borders of Israel-Palestine with fencing, mines and surveillance equipment.

H. Four border crossing points will be established in the vicinities of Jenin, Jerusalem, Hebron, and Gaza City.

I. Ten kilometers of Palestinian territory bordering Israel will be a demilitarized zone.

    J. Fifteen kilometers of Palestinian airspace bordering Israel
       will be Israeli airspace.

    K. Palestinian shipping will not come within twenty kilo-
       meters of Israeli waterspace, except for the Gaza where
       it will be ten kilometers.

    L. Palestine will assist Israel in its peace effort with the
       surrounding Arab states.

    M. Israel and Palestine will agree to semi-annual United
       Nations inspections of all borders.

VIII. The development of the Palestinian economy will be a
    central focus for the new government.

    A. The goal is to transfer the Palestinian dependence on
       the Israeli economy to a dependence on a new, vibrant
       Palestinian economy.

    B. The economic system of Palestine will be decided by
       the transitional government as either a market oriented
       or a centrally planned system.

    C. The transitional government will form the Palestine
       Economic Council (PEC) to oversee the development
       and protection of the economy.

       1. The PEC will be an appointed board of eleven.

       2. The PEC will recommend initiatives such as the
          establishment of a treasury, federal reserve, a tariff
          system, for example.

    D. Palestine will initiate a series of public and private
       work programs to build an effective infrastructure.

       1. A large harbor facility will be built in Gaza to en-
          courage export/import business.

       2. International airports will be constructed near the
          Dead Sea and the coast of Gaza to promote easy
          travel.

       3. A railroad/mass transit network will be established to
          connect all of Palestine for easy travel and the quick
          transport of products for export.

4. Palestine will promote and assist in the development of an industrial base.
5. Agricultural products will be promoted as a key Palestinian export to the Arab nations.
E. Palestine will issue a separate currency called the Palestinian dinar.
  1. Palestine will not honor the Israeli shekel.
  2. Israel will permit the use of both the dinar and shekel in East Jerusalem.
F. Palestinian labor may continue to work in Israel for one year after the formation of the transitional government.
  1. Palestinian labor must shift its focus toward the building of Palestine's economy and infrastructure.
  2. Israel will integrate the new Jewish immigrants into their labor force.
G. Economic assistance and investment from abroad will be encouraged, but monitored for destabilizing influences.
H. No Jewish or Israeli investment will be permitted in Palestine for a fifty year period, subject to extension.
I. Joint business ventures will be promoted between Palestinian and Israeli industries.

IX. Israel and Palestine will sponsor an annual conference on regional water and mineral disputes.

  A. Israel and Palestine agree not to alter, pollute, or halt the flow of rivers and streams.
  B. Israel and Palestine will sell/trade water and mineral rights at fair market prices.

X. A series of goodwill agreements will be enacted to create a peaceful atmosphere between Israel and Palestine.

  A. Israel and Palestine will be referred to as the "Brother States of the Holy Land."
  B. Israel will provide technical assistance to Palestine on the building of harbors and airports.
  C. Palestine will host a series of cultural/economic educational programs.

XI. Peace, justice and security will be a reality for the Israelis and Palestinians once they agree to the terms of this proposal.

    A. Israel will realize peace, but also a high level of security with the creation of Palestine in this manner.

    B. Palestinians will finally have their peace with Israel, but justice more importantly, with the fulfillment of Palestinian self-determination.

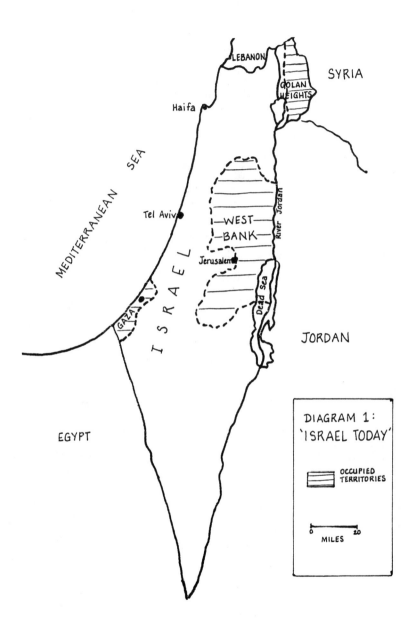

LEBANON

SYRIA

GOLAN
HEIGHTS

Haifa

MEDITERRANEAN SEA

Tel Aviv

WEST
BANK

River Jordan

Jerusalem

I S R A E L

Dead Sea

GAZA

JORDAN

EGYPT

DIAGRAM 1:
'ISRAEL TODAY'

OCCUPIED
TERRITORIES

0   20
MILES

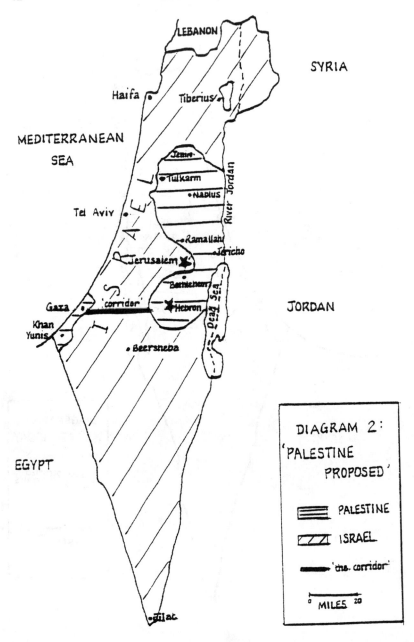

DIAGRAM 2:
'PALESTINE PROPOSED'

- PALESTINE
- ISRAEL
- 'the corridor'

0 MILES 20

PALESTINE

DIAGRAM 3:
'TWO STATE SOLUTION'
PALESTINE & ISRAEL
0   MILES 20

ISRAEL

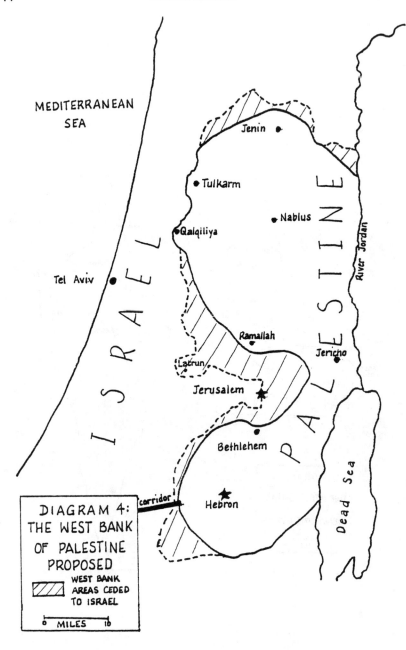

MEDITERRANEAN
SEA

Jenin

Tulkarm

Nablus

Qalqiliya

ISRAEL

Tel Aviv

PALESTINE

River Jordan

Ramallah

Jericho

Latrun

Jerusalem

Bethlehem

Dead Sea

corridor

Hebron

DIAGRAM 4:
THE WEST BANK
OF PALESTINE
PROPOSED

WEST BANK
AREAS CEDED
TO ISRAEL

0 MILES 10

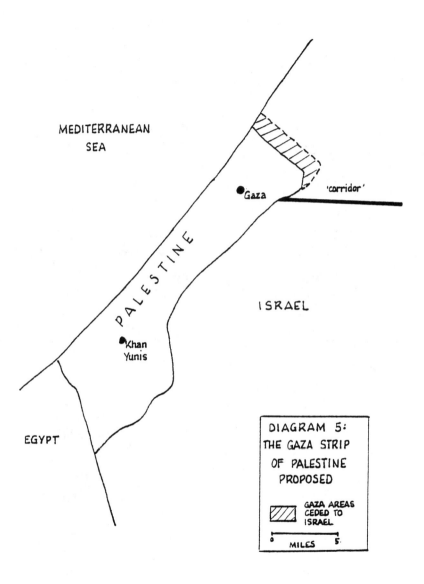

MEDITERRANEAN
SEA

●Gaza

'corridor'

PALESTINE

ISRAEL

●Khan
Yunis

EGYPT

DIAGRAM 5:
THE GAZA STRIP
OF PALESTINE
PROPOSED

GAZA AREAS
CEDED TO
ISRAEL

0   5
MILES

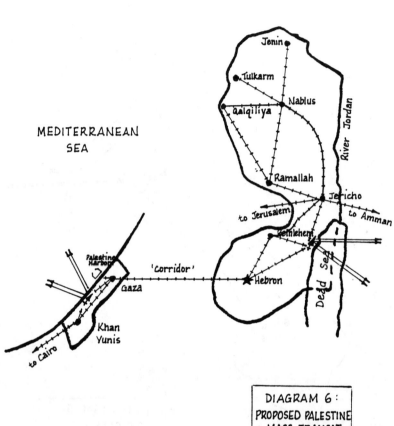

DIAGRAM 6:
PROPOSED PALESTINE
MASS TRANSIT
SYSTEM
Railroad
Airport
Flight Paths
Harbor
MILES

Chapter 7

Sharing the Land?

"God brings men into deep waters, not to drown them, but to cleanse them." —Aughey

The often criticized 1947 United Nations Partition Plan of Palestine was likely the best solution to a very complicated problem. The partition would have formed two states, one for the Jews and one for the Palestinian Arabs. Jerusalem would have been an international city under the control of neither Arab nor Jew. Unfortunately, the 1948 Arab-Israeli war and its aftermath omitted one partner in the partition plan, the Palestinian Arabs. The only lasting solution is to fulfill the 1947 U.N. Partition, not on the terms of 1947, but on terms acceptable today. The peace proposal in *Chapter 6* outlines a two-state solution on modified terms that both can accept. Some will approve of this proposal, others will reject it, but more importantly, people will begin thinking about this and other plans for achieving peace.

Until recently, the lack of willingness toward compromise and sacrifice by both peoples delayed the prospect of peace indefinitely. The intransigence of both the Israeli and Palestinian leadership resulted in widespread frustration and the outbreak of the Palestinian Intifada. In fact, the stalemate incited the radical groups (Hamas, Islamic Jihad, Temple Mount Faithful, Kach, for example) and increased their membership.

The Israelis have maintained two central positions that have prevented a peaceful settlement with the Palestinians. The first is that the Palestinian Arabs do not have the right to self determination. The second is that the occupied territories can be controlled indefinitely. This takes us back to the issue of justice and the protection of people's inherent rights. Israel must accept the fact that the Palestinians do have the right to self-determination, just as the Israelis themselves do. By doing so, they not only move closer to peace, but affirm the Israeli commitment to justice. Israel's first prime minister, David Ben-Gurion, once said that Israel would survive, "only if it maintains its moral, spiritual, and intellectual standards." A double standard concerning peoples' inherent rights is not a solid foundation for a legitimate state. A Palestinian state is not just an option, but a necessity for peace.

Furthermore, Israel is deceiving itself with the belief that it can control the occupied territories indefinitely. The high Palestinian population growth rate coupled with the heightening tensions in the territories will eventually result in a violent backlash against the Israelis. Israel's maintaining the *status quo* in the territories is equivalent to leaving a case of gangrene alone in the hope it will heal itself. Gangrene will spread and kill just as the Palestinian problem will. The only option is to eliminate the infected areas and for Israel, this means releasing the occupied territories. The Gaza-Jericho First Autonomy plan is evidence that the Israelis have realized that something must be done with the occupied territories.

Likewise, the Palestinians have held two positions that the Israelis would not accept. The first is that Jerusalem must be not only a part of Palestine, but its capital. The second is that the PLO is the sole representative of the Palestinian people.

The Palestinians overwhelmingly favor a divided Jerusalem where the eastern part of the city would become the capital of Palestine. If this is unattainable, they then favor Jerusalem as an international city under administration by the United Nations. Few Palestinians favor the idea of relinquishing the whole city to Israel. The Palestinian community is eighty-eight percent Sunni Muslim and twelve percent Christian. Jerusalem is the third most important holy site in Islam, and the first in Christianity. It is a city of the utmost religious and historical importance to all Palestinians.

Jerusalem was initially founded by the Jews and remains the most important city to Judaism. When Israel conquered the eastern half of Jerusalem in 1967, it was quickly annexed and proclaimed the unified capital of Israel. Since 1967, the Israelis have vigorously increased the Jewish population of Jerusalem through the development of the city itself and the establishment of Jewish settlements on the surrounding hills. The population of Jerusalem today is approximately five-hundred and fifty thousand of which four-hundred thousand are Jews and one-hundred and fifty thousand are Palestinian. The Palestinians argue that this population growth was a concerted Israeli effort to Judaicize the city. Moreover, they claim it was done in open violation of International Law by building Jewish settlements on occupied lands and then redistricting the city to include those settlements. There is in fact truth to this claim, but it is also a fact that the population of Jerusalem has consistently had a Jewish majority since the 1880's. And more importantly, on the eve of Israel's creation in 1947 the population of Jerusalem was nearly one-hundred and sixty-five thousand, of which one-hundred thousand were Jews, thirty-five thousand were Muslims, and thirty thousand were Christians. To the Israeli citizen, Jerusalem is the Jewish city which represents Israel to the world. Neither Labor nor Likud will ever be party to any sacrifice regarding Jerusalem, for it would be political suicide. Jerusalem is not a negotiable item.

For forty years, the Palestinians refused to acknowledge Israel's right to exist, but in 1988, and again in 1993, they gave in on this issue out of necessity. To get statehood, the Palestinians will eventually have to submit on the issue of Jerusalem as well. It is far better to do it now when it can still be used as a significant bargaining chip. Twenty years from now Jerusalem will have one million Jews and only two-hundred and fifty thousand Palestinians. It will no longer be an issue. The Israelis will be far more flexible on Palestinian statehood if they are assured of their status in Jerusalem. In September 1993, in the midst of the historic mutual recognition agreement, PLO Chairman Yasir Arafat was quoted saying, "The Palestinian state is within our grasp. Soon the Palestinian flag will fly on the walls, the minarets and the cathedrals of Jerusalem." Statements of this nature do considerable harm, for they fulfill the fears of Israel and harden the Israeli position against Palestinian statehood. The Palestinians must be willing to accept a state without Jerusalem in exchange for free access and the protection of all their interests in the Holy City. It is preferable to have a state without Jerusalem, while knowing your interests there are protected, than not to have any state. These are the only two options available to the Palestinians. They should seize the opportunity of statehood, even if it is not everything they want, for it gives them the legitimacy they both desire and deserve.

Since the creation of the Palestine Liberation Organization (PLO) in 1964, the Israelis have refused to acknowledge it as the legitimate representative of the Palestinian people. To the Israelis, open negotiation with PLO was equivalent to defeat and humiliation. In August-September 1993, in a surprising move, Israel publicly admitted to secret negotiations with the PLO on the Gaza-Jericho Autonomy Plan. Moreover, Israel formally recognized the PLO as the representative of the Palestinian people. This is an historic breakthrough on one of the most confrontational issues, for the legitimate leaders of both peoples can now negotiate at the same table.

In creating the State of Palestine, there are two key questions that must be asked. First, does the formation of Palestine place unmanageable risk on Israel?

Currently in the occupied territories there are nearly two million Palestinians, many of whom are active at subverting the occupation. Israel is faced with large scale security risks from the territories: the Intifada, the terrorist attacks, and the attacks on Israeli citizens. Would the risk be any greater if the occupied territories were the separate nation of Palestine? Clearly it would be more difficult to monitor the movement of terrorists and offensive weaponry, but this can be minimized through proper security agreements. In fact, the security threat emanating from the territories should diminish. After all, prior to 1967 Israel was not faced with serious security threats from the West Bank or Gaza Strip. The significant threat came from Syria's Golan Heights. The creation of Palestine will separate the Palestinians from the Israeli military/citizenry and this will quickly serve to lessen the tensions. The borders will have to be closely monitored for terrorist infiltration, but this is no different than the current surveillance on the Jordanian border. With a nation of their own, the Palestinians will no longer be struggling to defeat a military occupation.

Secondly, will the formation of Palestine without Jerusalem satisfy the Palestinians? Both the Israelis and Palestinians must be content with the boundaries of each state. It is vital that the Palestinians are able to accept this agreement and keep to it. If there is any hint that the Palestinians will try to reopen the issue of Jerusalem, the Israelis will resist a settlement. Therefore, the Palestinians must be sure that they can make this important sacrifice. If they are given a nation along with open access to Jerusalem and protection of their interests there, would they not seize the opportunity? After ample rhetoric to the contrary, I believe they would.

If the Israelis come to view the state of Palestine as a significant security risk, they will always be able to consider the back door escape of reoccupying her. The Palestinians know this all too well and will work over a period of time to eliminate and defuse any tensions with Israel. The Palestinians know that they would be no match for the well experienced Israeli military.

By allowing the creation of Palestine, the Israelis do take a significant risk because they legitimize both Palestine and the Palestinian people. If Israel were forced to reoccupy, she would surely come under intense pressure from the world community. It is infrequent that Israel would bow to world opinion anyway, though. Israel would risk the potential of U.N. sanctions and/or an Arab assault aimed at defending the Palestinians. On the positive side, the Israelis would be viewed as a just nation that allowed the Palestinians their opportunity at statehood. If it doesn't work, at least Israel will be seen as the tolerant society that took a chance in the name of justice.

Jorge (Mullen) - 1994 oil on canvas.
Road to the Holy Land

Jorge (Mullen) - 1993 oil on canvas.
The Search for Justice

Jorge (Mullen) - 1993 oil on canvas.
People Without A Homeland

Destroyed Egyptian tank in the Negev Desert of Israel. Photo: Mullen (1986).
Peace with Hands, No More Fighting with Arms!

Jorge (Mullen) - 1993 oil on canvas.
Neighbor Confronts Neighbor

Jorge (Mullen) - 1994 oil on canvas.
Coming to Terms with Oneself

Photo: Mullen (1987).

Jerusalem

Chapter 8

The Moshe-Hassan Dialogue

"When your neighbor's house is afire your own property is at stake." —Horace

The majority of the proposed peace settlement in Chapter 6 was obtained from the following two day conversation in Jerusalem between a prominent Jew (*Moshe*) and a Palestinian Arab (*Hassan*). Their agreements, disagreements, and compromises are the basis for the peace proposal. It is worthwhile reading the conversation to see how two reasonable people with opposing views can bridge their differences through dialogue.

Moshe emigrated to Palestine from Eastern Europe in 1938. He is a former Israeli Defense Forces (IDF) colonel with combat experience in the Sinai Campaign (1956), the Six-Day War (1967), and the Yom Kippur War (1973). In 1976 he resigned his IDF position to seek a career in politics. Today, in his late fifties, he is an official of the Labor Party. He is married, has three children, and resides in the Tel Aviv suburb of Tzahala.

Hassan was born and raised in a small farming village in the coastal plain north of Tel Aviv. In the 1948 war, he and his family fled to a refugee camp near Nablus. He was educated in England in political philosophy and is a supporter of Arafat's Fatah faction

GEORGE MULLEN

Neighbor Confronts Neighbor
by Jorge (Mullen) - 1993 oil on canvas

of the P.L.O. Currently, he is a university professor in the West Bank. He is fifty-three years old, married, has five children and two grandchildren.

The names of *Moshe* and *Hassan* have been changed to ensure their personal safety.

Setting:

West Jerusalem, in a small flat overlooking the Old City of Jerusalem and the Mount of Olives.

Dialogue:

Meeting with an Israeli Jew and a Palestinian Muslim, *Moshe* and *Hassan*, respectively. The topic of discussion is the possibility of an Israeli-Palestinian peace settlement and what it would entail.

Day One

Hassan: "I wish we were meeting under better conditions, but that seems to be the fate of our peoples. I'm shocked, to say the least, that a man of your Zionist military background would agree to meet with a man such as myself. You have my promise that your part in this conversation will remain unknown just as I would like my part unknown. Neither one of us would ever want known, at this point of our lives, that we've been meeting together about such issues."

Moshe: "Good to meet you, but the pleasure is mine, for we must look beyond ourselves to see if peace is possible for us and our peoples. I pray that there is, and that is why time was made to discuss this to help George and to find out in my mind. As for this conversation you have my promise on silence."

George: "A couple of background questions first, and then we'll proceed to the main dialogue. I'd like each of you to describe your experiences regarding the Israeli-Palestinian conflict, including your feelings past and present, Hassan?"

Hassan: "Well, it is a very difficult question, George. We look back and see so many years of blood, so many years of hate, so many years of humiliation. It's hard to look back, but I'll try. I was a young boy, eight years old, when the great disaster occurred in

1948. As you know, the United Nations partitioned Palestine and as the Jews declared their independence, our Arab armies attacked. With my family, we were a modest family living in the coastal plain north of Jaffa as farmers. We didn't have much money, but my father was a well respected man about the village. As the war came, our family, like so many others . . . we fled to what is the West Bank, to the area near Nablus thinking we would be able to return once the fighting ended. The word of Zionist inspired massacres at Deir Yassin and elsewhere terrified us so we packed up and left. To this day, I remember my mother sobbing. I think she knew more than my father about our future with those tears.

"Like my father and our neighbors we thought we would be able to return in a short time. I honestly remember that! But, unfortunately for my people, the Jews made a physical decision not to allow our return. Our houses were looted, our land stolen, we were abandoned! When we fled we left everything behind except a small baggage of clothing and the little money we had. Everything was stolen . . . our land, our animals, our family history, books, everything!

"I ended up growing up in Nablus in a refugee camp, where my family still lives. 1948 aged my parents fifteen years in six months. Everything lost and forced to live in a camp waiting to return. My father was well respected and hardworking and was able to feed and clothe us and even put money away for education. Because of this, I and two brothers were able to receive education in England. We are the fortunate ones. I have studied our situation in depth for many years and have spoken at many universities in Europe. I have always been a critic of Zionism and the Jews for what they had done to my father and to my family . . . for I could physically see my father age overnight, literally! It was devastating to lose everything—land, animals, memories, everything gone. Except the few things that we carried. Everything else was gone.

"With every new Zionist treachery, as Sinai (1956) or the 1967 War, we would scream 'Zionist pigs,' and realize our dream of returning home was rapidly disappearing. And the Zionist terrorist activity to Palestinians has been endless—Deir Yassin in 1948, Qibya in 1953, Kfar Kassem in 1956, Sabra and Shatila in

1982, to mention only a few. Sharon and Eitan[1] live to create Palestinian death and hardship!

"My parents died in the early 1970's, crushed by disappointment at never returning to my father's land, which was my grandfather's land before him. As time has passed, one tends to become softer. But for me, especially after my father's death. The sore point had gone. We had learned to hate the Jews. They were the reason for our misery. But now I'm a middle-aged man, I like to think I'm young, but I'm not. Please disagree with me! (laughing)"

Moshe: "Age is Wisdom."

Hassan: "In these battles and confrontations in the camps I have known too many that have died or been deported. And in Lebanon the misery has been greater. And at this point I really do not want to see this killing go on. There must be point for compromise. Twenty years ago I would have said the only solution was to push the Jew into the sea and the dismantling of the Zionist state. But now it is a different situation. I've seen my family hurt by it and I know the Jews have seen their families hurt by it. We must find a compromise, a middle ground, so the fighting can end. That is my dream!

"The fact of the matter is, I think the Jews and Palestinian people are much the same. The peoples themselves I think are very much the same. I'm not sure why, but we are. Both of us are arrogant, I'd say very hardworking and we all want a higher education and seek the higher professions available. We (the Palestinians) are the most successful of the Arab peoples. Our people are well educated and have been great successes throughout the world. From running corporations in America to leading professors in Europe. Both our peoples are very successful, arrogant and stubborn. And most of all, we both want the land of Palestine. I see the similarities and so do you. It drives both of us crazy. I've talked too much, sorry."

---

[1] Both General Ariel Sharon and General Rafael Eitan are members of the Knesset (Congress) and are considered to be vehemently anti-Arab.

George: "And you, Moshe."

Moshe: "I also was young when the war started. I emigrated from Poland with my family. English became my main language for some time. I remember little Polish, for my parents refused it to be spoken. Hebrew became our language, but English was useful in dealing with the British Administration. My brother and sister and myself also became familiar with English out of necessity. We ran errands for the Brits on our bikes for two mils each here and there. Our family depended on the additional money we could get. Although it was very little.

"I was a young teen when Israel became a nation and I take great pride in our nation and what we have done. My nation has won many wars, we have made deserts bloom through irrigation. We have done more with this land than the Palestinians ever could have."

Hassan: "But does that give you the right to take our land!"

Moshe: "I didn't mean to provoke. The last thing I want is to argue. I am trying to describe my background and attitude."

Hassan: "Go on, I didn't intend to. . . "

Moshe: "But I also have pain in my heart. I had long been a military man before entering the political field. I had been one of the greatest supporters of Israel and the policy towards the Palestinians. In my view the true Palestine was Jordan. Jordan makes up much of the British Palestine mandate and some seventy-five percent of the people are Palestinian. Jordan should be Palestine. Now I know that is not true. Our young people are the most staunch supporters on both sides. When I was young, I was much more staunch. I hated the Palestinians. Now I just want to see the killing end and I tell you where I saw the killing come close to home. I have been in many wars and seen many people die, but here about three years ago one of my son's closest friends, a young Sabra that I knew very well, seen through my son's entire life, a good boy . . . he was killed in Gaza on patrol by a knife in the lung. I wanted to see heads roll for this. The trash, the dog Palestinians, how can they do such a thing? Well now, after a time, I have moderated and I thought, you know, we created this situation. Me, the other people that run this country, and the Palestinians that control their terror groups. We are killing these children. I do not want my son and my son's children to inherit this continual problem of hate, mistrust and killing! I want to see it end, in a way where the Palestinians are happy, the Israelis are happy, and the killing can end. It may never all end, but I think there is something to do to reduce it.

"I said I have always been one of the most staunch anti-Palestinian people. But I think at some point you have to wake up, smell the roses, and make a decision for the betterment of your family and your people. And that is why I think it is worthwhile talking with Hassan on the peace issue. But that does not mean I have joined the Peace Now movement! As for Hassan saying that the Israelis and Palestinians are very much the same, in some ways yes, some no. Some very disturbing things bother me about that similarity. As we call the Palestinians, I mean the Palestinian people, terrorists, we describe them as dogs. But there are terrorists, there are many terrorist groups—the PLO, Popular Front and all the other radical factions that kill Israelis, or Americans for that matter. But one must compare that to, one must look at the Israeli history. When this nation was being developed there were radical factions of Jews killing Arabs and British in an effort to create this great nation."

Hassan: "And there are Jews today doing the same!"

Moshe: "Menachim Begin and the Irgun itself were directly involved in the destruction of Deir Yassin, which Hassan brought up. In addition, Begin and his group were firsthand, and Yitzak Shamir to point out a name, were firsthand involved in the destruction of the King David Hotel in Jerusalem, killing hundreds. These facts are humiliating to me for they are no better than Arafat blowing up planes. In many ways I respect these men, not for these actions, but for what they did because they created this nation. They successfully defeated six Arab armies that greatly outnumbered us in 1948.

"But we must get beyond this and see that all Palestinians are not terrorists, all Israelis are not terrorists, and all Israelis are not killing Palestinians in Lebanon. I want to see the peace process go forward, not at the Israeli's expense. Preferably at the Palestinian's expense. But it must move forward."

George: "With this in mind how can a lasting peace be achieved between the Israelis and Palestinians? Hassan, please. . . "

Moshe: "No simple answer!"

Hassan: "Well I tell you, for many years, like I said, we called for to drive the Jew into the sea, you know the Arabs . . . Nasser and his men scheming to drive the Jews into the sea and we got caught up in that euphoria. That is old now. We've even seen President Arafat and the PLO officially recognize the State of Israel. What the Palestinians need, my people, need, is our own state. I am not calling for the destruction of Israel and the creation of Palestine in what is now Israel. What we do want is a nation that we can be proud of. United Nations Council Resolutions 242 and 338 demand the right of self-determination for the Palestinian people.

"As long as the hate builds in the camps, the destruction, the anti-Zionist slogans, nothing good can come of this. Nothing good! Our people need something we can take pride in, something we can build, something we can work for, something we can have an experience at building a new country. And that is where we will become a very very successful people and we will leave the Jews alone. We will have something to work for, something to take pride in. The refugee camps are a hotbed of disease and hate and they will not help anything. The Intifada is the result of this desperation of my people. As the young face your trained occupiers with stones and slogans . . . we both know it is from the heart. The Jews cannot win by occupation. We must get past this stage. What I think is the only solution, is for not limited autonomy for the Palestinians, but a separate state. Meaning a sovereign state in the West Bank and Gaza! I think that will give the Palestinian people a source of pride. Palestinians will move back home to build this state. There are many things that can be done. So many ways people can have an impact.

"The freedom fighters you call terrorists will lose their reason for being terrorists. They will opt to return to Palestine to build our country. What I'm saying is, there must be a state of Palestine for the fighting to end. It is the only way, it is the only just way for us to protect our peoples. Our soldiers of liberation will change their vision of destroying Israel to building a state of our own (Palestine)!

"After all, the Jew is illegally occupying the West Bank, Gaza, Golan, and parts of Lebanon. United Nations resolutions 242 and 338 have demanded your withdrawal, but you have not moved a single step. The McMahon Papers[2] have been forgotten. We have been betrayed by the British, the Americans, the United Nations and even our Arab brothers. Our Arab brothers led by Abdullah and Hussein helped us by annexing what remained of our land left from the Jews! King Hussein has never helped us to establish our own state on the Jordan. He is more concerned with appeasing Jewish interests and saving his own neck.

"The injustice done to the Palestinians mandates, in the eyes of Allah, that man must correct this injustice. Our own state, though not perfect, will begin to right a wrong. There must be international legitimacy to any settlement."

George: "Moshe?"

Moshe: "Like I said, for many many years I always called Jordan the Palestinian state. If you do not like it here move to Jordan, if you do not like it in Gaza, move to Jordan, if you do not like it in Judea, move to Jordan. That has never been, never ever been fair and I know that. These people have a right to land, though we cannot share this land of Israel. I think that what must be done, I have to agree with Hassan on this. A nation of

---

[2] The McMahon Papers consist of the correspondence between Sherif Hussein, speaking for the Arabs, and Sir Henry McMahon, of England, during WWI. In exchange for Arab participation in Britain's war against Turkey, the British promised to recognize Arab independence.

Palestine must be created now, in a limited degree, there are many conditions with that, but in the territories of Judea, Samaria and Gaza. A separate nation of Palestine will help start defusing the problem. I am talking about the lands that have not been annexed. Many ways I worry about the timing, I am very security conscious. After all, I spent many years in military administration . . . The Iraqi Aggression next door is an example of our fear. But security can only be carried so far."

Hassan: "Israel had no problem from 1948 to 1967 with the West Bank and Gaza under Arab control. The Golan was your only real threat and that is an issue for Syria, not us. The West Bank and Gaza were not a security threat, only in your mind they were."

Moshe: "I think the security problems will tend to dissipate in Lebanon and the territories once Palestine is created. And I must say this Intifada will die at some point, nothing will come of it, but it will rise again another day. That is what I fear, that my children and grandchildren will be dealing with this. The Intifada may be forcing our hand . . . I hope your children keep up the pressure until a settlement is achieved.

"If a Palestine is created and does not work and the security risk to Israel increases, I pray for you. For a big gamble it is. Arik (Sharon) and the likes of Meir Kahane will have their way and the Palestinian population will be transferred across the Jordan, forever!"

Hassan: "I am shocked to hear you agree. It is rare indeed for a Jew and Palestinian to agree on anything, let alone such talk that will be seen as treasonous by your fellow Jews."

George: "Now if we both agree that there is no chance of peace until the Palestinians have a homeland, then what are the main obstacles to achieving this homeland? Why has nothing been done? Hassan?"

Hassan: "Well, you know, it's those who don't want to give it up! And I think this is the main point. The Jews have the West Bank, they have Gaza, they have the Golan, they don't want to give it up. Maybe for security reasons, maybe because they have it, why should they give it up? The Zionists certainly are not concerned with Palestinian well-being. They fought for it and they may think they deserve it. I'm not going to get into the Zionist thing thinking the Jews want to take all of Jordan also. Although many of the settlers I'm sure do. But I think they feel comfortable. The government is very very hard-line and I don't think they ever will give up land. The haves do not want to give to the have-nots. I think this is the main point."

George: "Moshe, would you address this question?"

Moshe: "I think, a Palestinian homeland really is the only way to defuse the problem or to start to defuse the problem. The obstacles to a peace process are many. But I really hold the responsibility, not with the Labor Party, not with the Likud Party, but with the radical fringe groups that control our government. More important, our government system is the problem. Our government is a coalition government, as you know, George. In order to maintain a majority, our government has been forced to form a coalition to maintain power. For the Likud Party to take power they had to make arrangements with the Haredi religious parties such as Tehiya. These religious parties are the ones that want to settle the territories. They believe in the ancient areas of Judea, Samaria and Gaza and in resettling those areas with Jews and transferring out the Palestinians. They never want these lands to be given up. These are the most dangerous people in our government. Because they control our government through minority. The religious parties may be ten percent of our population, but they control forty percent of the population by forming a coalition with Likud, and in turn they control 100 percent of our nation's policies by holding veto power. Likud cannot move in fear of offending these religious fanatics. If they do, the coalition falls apart, and then Labor bends back, makes arrangements with the Haredi parties and then Labor cannot move.

"The majority in Israel do not want a Palestinian nation, but the issue cannot even be brought up because of the Haredi religious fanatics. And I point out that many of these religious fanatics do not serve in the Israeli Army as is required for so called religious reasons! These extremist parties are the main problem to creating a peace settlement. Neither Labor or Likud can chance compromise without their support."

Hassan: "The real problem is your system of government for allowing the extremists such power through veto. You need to change it."

Moshe: "I agree! But it is very hard to change now."

George: "With these facts in mind let's begin with the main dialogue. Let us assume that each of you is the sole representative of your people. You are finally together to discuss a peace settlement that will satisfy both the Israeli and Palestinian populace. If you can achieve a detailed peace agreement it will be enacted. If not, the *status quo* will remain. The Intifada will continue; the killing, mistrust, and hate between Israeli and Palestinian will carry on! Hassan, please begin."

Hassan: "Now, in the development of peace, like I stated I think it is necessary Moshe, for this . . . a Palestinian homeland. And I think the discussion must take a turn here to evolve how that homeland can come about. Because we do not want some sort of limited autonomy under Jewish control. It must be a fully independent Palestinian state, where we can build the pride in our state and I think that is the important factor. I'm not sure you understand. . . "

Moshe: "Yes, I agree, but there is much to do to get to that point."

Hassan: "Yes, and I do think that we must work at it very hard because, sure, we could not just immediately create a state of Palestine, but I do not want to see it go half way to a limited autonomy under Jewish hegemony and then, disappear and that be it. What I want, is if we are to do this discussion, is to develop a full Palestinian sovereignty under a Palestinian state under a Palestinian flag alongside a Jewish state."

Moshe: "I agree, but many details need be worked out."

Hassan: "Well, you know, the others think that these have to be negotiations! There has to be give and take from both sides, compromise, we have to be able to come up with a settlement that both Palestinian and Jew alike would be able to accept. It cannot be you issuing yes or no, yes or no, it has to be something we both find mutually acceptable. You understand what I mean?"

Moshe: "Well if we. . . "

Hassan: "I mean, you are in the position of strength. If it is solely up to you, you can dictate the yes or no, the conditions. That is not the spirit of negotiation or compromise!"

Moshe: "Now, we have the land, and because we do, we are the ones with the security risk. We are the haves, as you said. We control the administered territories! We are the ones that will have to set the conditions! I want to work with you so that it is mutually acceptable, but we are the administrators and there is no way my people will accept a peace that is not in the spirit of the true peace. And that is the problem. So we will be setting the conditions . . . not so much because I want to, but because I have to. My people must accept it!"

Hassan: "And my people too and that is the fact. I mean if we give up too much in return for a homeland, you know. What your conditions are I do not know, but if they are treacherous my people will not accept. I will be assassinated and it will be a disaster for both our peoples! For the fact that you've even accepted a Palestinian state in theory will put the ball in roll . . . if you understand what I say?"

Moshe: "Yes, of course I understand. We are both in a questionable situation if things break down."

Hassan: "The negotiations must be in a spirit of justice, not one-sided! Resolutions 242 and 338 have already mandated such action. Let us correct the injustice done to my people! (The Palestinians)"

Moshe: "Hassan, we both know 242 and 338 were paper resolutions to appease you Arabs in pains of defeat. There is no weight in the United Nations! It is up to us and no outsider opinion makes a difference."

Hassan: "I don't agree, you know, but it is irrelevant. We need not get bogged down with this. So Moshe, why don't you initiate our negotiations on how you see a peaceful way we can create this Palestinian state?"

Moshe: "Yes, now, I have spent much time in the military administration and in the Labor Party. So I think I know quite a bit about what needs to be done for the people. What the Israeli citizen will accept and I believe I have a feeling for what the Palestinians will accept. I sketched out a few notes here on things that need be addressed and how they can be achieved. I will start to go through with them and we can discuss each point one by one.

"The first point is that of the actual creation of Palestine. Now I accept in theory a nation of Palestine in the areas of Judea, Samaria and Gaza. Not the Golan! The Golan will not be given up, absolutely not! So lets not make that an issue."

Hassan: "That is the business of Syria."

Moshe: "Good. . . But let us go through a few of the transitional points, because we cannot just create Palestine. There has to be a transitional government that takes control. This is what I put forth . . . I think there should be a four year transitional government of Palestine. We have general Palestinian elections six months from today to elect a president, and a one hundred-representative Knesset, congress-type of body to govern. The elected governing body in the four year period develops a constitution, a set of laws, and everything else you will need to govern Palestine . . . while still under Israeli administration. . . "

Hassan: "You mean occupation!"

Moshe: "May I go forth?. . . The most important thing is that there can, for my people to accept, for me to accept it . . . that there must be no, no, no PLO involvement and no persons in detention! The jails remain until the government is established. No PLO is accepted, no Palestinian from outside the occupied territories is accepted, that is very important. For four years, this is what we are asking. After the four years, any person, for this you set your own rules. For any person that has returned to live in Palestine has the right to run for office—a democratic society.

"So what you must do is elect your four-year government to set up your nation . . . a democratic nation with a president, a congress and what else you may seek. But it must be a real democracy, the first in the Arab world."

Hassan: "We would have it no other way. We are a democratic people."

Moshe: "Once this Palestinian government has been formed, has taken action, and has created a constitution and laws, then the Israeli withdrawal begins. At no less than year three of the transition, and no more than four years. Over a six month period we withdraw everything, plus whatever we have built if we so choose . . . industry hardware and so forth. All will be withdrawn. With no Palestinian interference or celebration until we are gone!"

Hassan: "Well I think you're right, there has to be a transitional government. But I'm not sure I agree with you on some of the issues. For one, the PLO is the sole representative of our people and the Palestine National Congress (PNC) is our parliamentary body . . . we do not need to create another!. . . . To exclude the PLO from this government would be political suicide for this new government. We cannot set a government and have it under attack from within, with forces within, to destroy it!"

Moshe: "Yes, but you do not understand. My people will never accept any Palestinian government that includes the PLO! My people see Arafat and your PNC as the source of the killing of Israeli children, blowing apart buses, we see them as the enemy. It is important they are not in the transition government . . . or any jailed persons of the PLO in the territories."

Hassan: "Well over sixteen thousand Palestinians currently are in so called detention for strictly political reasons. Many of these men are able leaders we want in our leadership."

Moshe: "That is unacceptable, unless they are due for release."

Hassan: "The Jews will make sure no one of value is freed!"

Moshe: "Maybe so."

Hassan: "What about, say, members that are known to be quite friendly to the PLO, actually members of the PLO, but living within the territories and are not in jail. I think they should be accepted to be involved in our government."

Moshe: "As long as they are not in jail I can accept that. I cannot accept Arafat and his thugs or Jabril or Habash[3] or any jailed individuals forming your government. Because it will be a sign to us that it will be a renegade government. We have to be very careful here! The government must come as strong, but not anti-Israeli. This is very important."

Hassan: "Well, the other point, I can agree with that! I can agree with that and I will go along with saying no jailed individuals until the government is formed. But I cannot agree that there will be no external Palestinians allowed to return to form our government! After all, only thirty percent of the Palestinian people live in the occupied territories. Nearly 3.5 million of our people live as refugees in squalid conditions of the camps in Jordan, Lebanon and throughout the world. These people have direct ties to us and deserve representation in our government. Because you exiled them does not mean they cannot be a part of us."

Moshe: "No! After the IDF withdraws anyone you chose can enter your government. But no person . . . from your so-called diaspora will be in the transition government!"

Hassan: "Once the transitional government is formed and is legislating we must have a policy that all Palestinians whether they live in Lebanon, Syria, Jordan, Tunisia, America . . . wherever the case may be, all Palestinians are welcome home! A free home under Palestinian protection. No more Jewish security once the government is formed."

---

[3] Ahmad Jabril—Leader, Popular Front for the Liberation of Palestine General Command (P.F.L.P-G.C), a radical anti-Arafat faction of the PLO.

George Habash—Leader, Popular Front for the Liberation of Palestine (P.F.L.P.), a radical faction of the PLO.

Both groups are considered highly dangerous.

Moshe: "That is your immigration policy. We will allow all Palestinians to enter except for the PLO leadership, Habash's Popular Front or any other known terror groups or militias coming from Lebanon and so forth. After we withdraw it is all your choosing. You may want to be careful on who and how many people you allow to immigrate. Large, sudden immigrations are difficult . . . we are learning with our Russian immigrants.

"More important, if Arafat were to return and rally your people to his cause, you could have a civil war within Palestine, still occupied by Israel. The Israelis and myself will not have the problem . . . we will be sending in the tanks and the occupation will go on. Arik (Sharon) will be more than happy to clear Judea and Samaria of all Palestinians . . . more pain to you!

"Once the transition government has stability, let's say all Palestinians are allowed to return, with the exception of the PLO and other terror groups, until we withdraw. After that it is your choice. You will be responsible for your immigration. Arafat and his thugs can return, but do not allow them to sacrifice your future."

Hassan: "If President Arafat or other known nationalists returned while the occupation still existed you would be tempted to seize them . . . so it does make sense."

Moshe: "We could have them a long time ago if we wanted them. Tunis is not so far, you know, for us!"

Hassan: "The transitional government, then, can include any non-jailed Palestinian in good standing from Gaza or the West Bank in free Palestinian elections. But we want foreign advisors to make sure the election is not interfered with. There must be no Jewish interference!"

Moshe: "Advisors . . . I agree, American."

Hassan: "No, United Nations Advisors. The bias of the United States is not welcome. The fifty billion dollars plus given to Israel by the Jewish lobby in Washington is not an action of an unbiased observer."

Moshe: "U.N. if you insist, but also American advisors."

Hassan: "Well, obviously, Palestinians of Jerusalem elected to our government will be honored."

Moshe: "No! Jerusalem in its entirety has been annexed by Israel. Those Palestinians in Jerusalem will not be represented in your government. If they want to take office then they must move to Palestine."

Hassan: "This is unacceptable!"

Moshe: "We will discuss the details to this in a few minutes when we discuss the border issues."

Hassan: "Okay, but there is much to say. In addition since all free citizens can seek office, then PLO faces and sympathizers will be elected. Faces as Faisal Husseini is one I'd like to see."

Moshe: "The more moderate, as Husseini, are acceptable, but Husseini would have to move his residence to Palestine first and renounce his ties to Jerusalem. His type would be pleasing to see. But it is up to you. The elected president and congress must be independent and not controlled from Tunis or Damascus! We will have our eye on this!"

Hassan: "Not stooges to Jewish interests."

Moshe: "Yes."

Hassan: "What of our universities, the civil administration, all our internal affairs? Do we take immediate control once our provisional government is elected?"

Moshe: "Good question, but no. After the provision government is elected there will be a six month waiting time. We do not want to overload your new government. After, let us say, six months our civil administration will begin handing over your affairs on a monthly basis. The first month we hand over all the schools and universities, the next month public works, the next water, electricity and sewage . . . the next food distribution, the next all police matters . . . and soon the judicial and prison control and finally national security . . . when the IDF withdraws . . . after the fourth year."

Hassan: "We want control as soon as is possible."

Moshe: "Agreed, and we will issue a list of dates of the civil matters being turned over to you. You will have time to pick teams of people to learn and control these affairs. In this way you will avoid a collapse of say, your water system or electricity. You will have time to focus on each detail. . . one at a time."

Hassan: "This is good! But I have a problem with the four year transitional government. I don't think it should be four years, I think maybe two years. At the end of two years, then we have general elections where President Arafat, his colleagues, or. . . "

Moshe: "No, do not call Arafat by the name of President! We are making an agreement here that the PLO leadership is not involved . . . Arafat is thus not your president. Your president is the man you elect to head your transition government."

Hassan: "Okay then, Mr. Arafat and his associates or anyone else, is allowed to gain power as president and congress after two years in a democratic election."

Moshe: "I disagree! I will agree to cutting the occupation to two years from the date of the creation of the Palestinian transition government. But if you have elections after the second year it could be a complete seizure of power by Arafat and his thugs and loss of democratic values in the nation of Palestine. It is important that Palestine be a democratic nation, as Israel . . . then we will be able to work together. If either become a dictatorship as the Arab nations are . . . Iraq and Syria are golden examples of this. If this were to happen to Palestine it would be a great danger to both of us. I do not think that is good."

Hassan: "What I'm saying when I say that after two years, we do not want the Israeli occupation to go for two more years once we have set up our transitional government. Let us put the Israeli occupation at six months, with a six month withdrawal . . . so you are out by one year. At two years we have general elections to. . . "

Moshe: "No, I must disagree! This is not a policy, we cannot quicken the system to make it better. It is better to make it slower . . . A longer system. Because there is much to do creating this Palestine. There should not be any immediate withdrawal. I think that is very important. I think general elections should be after four full years, once the transition government has had a long time to prove stability."

Hassan: "I get the feeling you're not negotiable on this point. Let us say this, let us do this. Let's put the occupation at eighteen months once the transitional government has been elected. At eighteen months a phased withdrawal is started so that all Jewish occupation forces, military administration, governmental bureaucracy, etc., etc., has been removed from the occupied territories by the first day of the second year."

Moshe: "Year three!"

Hassan: "Yes, I'm sorry. The first day of year three. So that after two full years the Jewish occupation will cease to be. And then it is up to us to declare general elections. I will say four years is too long, but you say two years is too short . . . so let us compromise on three years. General elections after three years . . . I think that is fair."

Moshe: "No!. . . Israel will be watching Palestine very close and your actions. If the transition government is shaky, looks like it may be toppled, or will call general elections early our occupation will continue. You must agree to four-year transition government and general elections every four years, as in America. No collapsing governments, as in Israel, no coalition government . . . but a system where elections occur regularly every four years. A system where we and the world can rely on it."

Hassan: "I see, you are preoccupied with the stability of our nation."

Moshe: "Yes!"

Hassan: "I will agree with the four year transitional government as long as you agree to complete withdrawal by day one, year three."

Moshe: "Agreed! Stability is what we must see. Four year transition government and four year terms show us that stability."

Hassan: "Additionally, after the four year transitional government ends our promise to you ceases. We can then choose what type of government we want . . . that is an internal affair. Who is to to say, George Habash could be elected president in our general election and may pursue a communist or socialist style government. I prefer democracy and that is most likely. But we do not want Jewish interference if we choose a government you do not find to your liking."

Moshe: "I understand, but I urge Palestine to remain a democracy. If an anti-Israeli dictatorship seizes power our involvement may be, unavoidable."

Hassan: "Then it is settled. After the four year transition we run our affairs as we so choose. And we will try to avoid any action that could provoke your army."

Moshe: "This one point is settled . . . there are many other points we have to discuss in creating this Palestine with which my family and my people can live. With the creation of Palestine, the Palestinian nation comes to exist one day after the transition government is formed. The nation of Palestine is created on that day.

"The transition government over the four-year period must develop a constitution, a full legislative body and a judicial system. Try and mirror it on the American or British system. Not some of the lesser quality systems as you see in the Arab nations. On the day of creation of Palestine a full peace agreement, treaty must be established with Israel. What I mean by a full peace treaty, I mean a complete peace treaty signed by the president, the first president of Palestine, and by the prime minister of Israel . . . accepted by both legislative bodies as a peace treaty. If it is not signed there will never be a withdrawal of Israeli Defense Forces, sad to say. What it must be, it must be a peace treaty with complete affirmation of the permanent borders of both Palestine and Israel and . . . we will get into the borders a bit later! Once we set up the borders of Palestine as the territories of Judea, Samaria, and Gaza and the borders of Israel where they are. Be in complete affirmation of the borders, including your affirmation of Israeli borders, including the Golan and our small security areas in South Lebanon. You will come under much pressure on these points, but it must be your

complete affirmation of the borders of Israel and the future borders of Palestine."

Hassan: "The Golan and Lebanon are not our business. That
must be discussed with Syria and Lebanon and the Druse for
that matter. Why should we be forced to recognize illegal borders
as those?"

Moshe: "If you do not, a Palestinian liberation terror group
for these areas may arise. We want complete affirmation on your
part of our existing borders."

Hassan: "Are you planning to annex your so-called security
zone in the ten kilometer zone of Lebanon?"

Moshe: "No comment."

Hassan: "Ah, I see."

Moshe: "In addition, in this peace treaty there must be an
outlawing of all terrorism and all PLO fringe groups directed
against Israel. You will work to reestablish all those refugee
camps in Lebanon, Jordan, Syria into your Palestinian nation and
to defuse all Palestinian front organizations as Habash's Popular
Front, the PLO and all others. All energy should be directed away
from the destruction of Israel to the building of Palestine.

"In addition, this peace treaty must include Palestine neutrality toward Israel. A permanent neutrality pact with Israel that any
time Israel gets involved in war with Syria, Lebanon, Jordan . . .
whatever nation it might be. The nation of Palestine remains neutral such as the Switzerland of the Middle East. You are the nation
of non-interference.

"In addition, you will declare a mutual defense treaty with
Israel declaring your obligatory right to assist Israel against
outside attack and you will not condone any attack on Israel!"

Hassan: "This peace treaty must be done in the words talking
of the Jewish State and Palestine as both brother states. It is time
we forget the terrible past and move into the future and begin to
consider ourselves brother states, two very small brother states in
a very large hostile Middle East, aimed at survival and helping
each other. As those words continue over time, people will start

to believe it and a brotherly relationship can then develop, as
before the Zionist movement.

"The treaty focuses on each one's role for peace. Not one-
sided, with the Jews dictating terms. If it is a mutually acceptable
peace treaty of partners I am all for it. For we have no desire or
intention of seeing further Zionist hostilities toward Palestinians."

Moshe: "Agreed."

Hassan: "Well, I think you have the right idea, on the peace
treaty because there must be a peace treaty with Israel. Because
we are going to continue to fear a reoccupation by Zionist forces
led by the likes of Shamir and Sharon. Your Jewish state clearly
is a superpower in terms of the Middle East. I suppose we'll get
to the military later. But that is to be the prime fear . . . is that
there could be a reoccupation of forces."

Moshe: "Absolutely. That is a fear. Because if we see any
problem our people will demand we enter Palestine. A reoccupation
will be the elimination of your Palestine. That is not our intention,
but the risk is there."

Hassan: "Well, you know, I think a peace treaty is appropri-
ate, but it has to be something that is not a humiliation of the
Palestinian people.

"I think the peace treaty must be a very obligatory instrument,
but one that won't humiliate the Palestinians . . . because our
people think the Jews are dictating to them. The peace must have
international legitimacy as well in representing Palestinians. If it
appears illegitimate the radical fringe groups will find support and
power. And that is what we don't want.

"We want to be on equal footing.I think that Palestinian
neutrality is good, I've no problem with that, after all our Arab
neighbors have done very little to help our cause . . . only
insomuch that it advances their position . . . look at Assad or the
likes of Sadat! We want to be able to defend ourselves. We will
not rely on the Jews! And we want in this treaty a promise by
Israel not to reoccupy Palestine ever again . . . and also a promise

of Israel to assist Palestine in the unlikely event of an attack by Syria or Jordan on Palestine."

Moshe: "That is acceptable and also, in it, it should be put that it is the responsibility of the Palestinian security forces and the IDF to prevent any border clashes. Clashes that can be taken as a border conflict which could result in war."

Hassan: "I agree, but the peace treaty, it must be in detail, it must be, must be accepted by our government, just as yours also."

Moshe: "This point is very important. If this peace treaty is not ratified by your Knesset (congress) for some minor point, it will not carry the weight I want. It is like the American President Wilson and his Fourteen Points of 1920, or what year it was, the American Congress did not ratify and it became nothing. It is what we do not want. We must have a ratified treaty . . ." (*Approximately thirty seconds of the conversation was drowned out by a small fender bender accident and argument on the street below*).

Hassan: "I agree wholeheartedly, but of course I cannot say, because I am not there, we don't have a legislative body, I don't know what can be passed or not."

Moshe: "You and I both know that something of this nature must be accepted. Our military administration will still be there!"

Hassan: "Now, hold on, that is poppycock. This brings up a good point! Just because the Zionist occupation forces are still here we do not want to be coerced into making settlements, doing things we don't want to do strictly because the occupation forces remain in our state. You are not to be dictating to us."

Moshe: "Yes, that point is understood."

Hassan: "Your occupation forces are here to keep peace until our government can take full control, and then things can be taken care of. We do not want you using that muscle, to flex and make so we do things your way. It must be done in a democratic way, but our way!"

Moshe: "I agree."

Hassan: "Go on, Moshe."

Moshe: "Next point is a tough point for me to bring up . . . because I cannot rely on you and I cannot rely on your people. I cannot rely on your people! Because it is a point of which neither you, nor any of your people have much control. But you will influence it! With this creation of, and formal peace treaty with, Palestine, we want peace with the Arabs. What I mean specifically is, we want formal peace treaties with Jordan and Saudi Arabia and as many other Arab states as possible. . . As Morocco and the Gulf Sheikdoms. A formal peace treaty!"

Hassan: "Well, you know, that's really not up to me, again. I mean that is, they are sovereign states. Those kingdoms, the kings they don't have to accept any peace . . . they may see risk from outside on this, from Iran or elsewhere to this. I absolutely cannot guarantee any such thing."

Moshe: "I know you cannot guarantee it, but we want your promise at effort in the treaty to help achieve peace between Jews and Arabs everywhere."

Hassan: "Well listen, I'll be frank with you, I think that with the creation of Palestine and a peace between our peoples, I think peace with Jordan will be very easy. King Hussein wants to make peace with Israel, but he cannot because you know, he's seen what happens with such men as Sadat . . . they get a bullet in the head. But I do think the King (Hussein) would be sympathetic. And I also think the Saudis would probably go along with it also. As long as they don't see great risk from the Islamic Republics such as Iran, and such. But Lebanon and Syria are a different game! Iraq . . . who knows."

Moshe: "Well, Lebanon before long will be part of Syria, we have known that for many years. Lebanon was a creation of France. Lebanon historically was always a part of greater Syria, at least in Assad's eyes. Syria will get control of Lebanon before long and we will keep control of our security area. I must say I do not want any promises from you toward Syria. We would like peace with Syria, but I know it is not going to come. We will deal with Syria on our own! When rockets were raining on Tiberius and the Galilee, in those days, we remember, it will not be the same! We will deal with Syria and that snake Assad in our own way. We would like peace with Syria, but do not require it.

"But I do require Palestinian promises to attain peace with Jordan and Saudi Arabia. The reason being, we have a peace with Egypt and we think the peace will last, especially with the creation of Palestine. A peace with Saudi Arabia, a peace with Jordan, will leave one border at risk and that would be Greater Syria. If we only had to watch that one border . . . we watch all our borders at all times, do not get me wrong! But this will mean only one border of true conflict."

Hassan: "Saudi Arabia does not share a border with you."

Moshe: "True, but it is very close and could be used as a base against us from the Red Sea."

Hassan: "Well, I think that you have my word that once the state of Palestine is created, we will work at attaining the peace once the occupation is over. Because they're not going to discuss peace until the occupation is over, until they're sure it will happen. But I believe we can work with you on King Hussein and Fahd and you'll get your peace. If Abdullah succeeds Fahd it may be a bit more difficult. He is hardheaded compared to Fahd."

Moshe: "Good, good."

Hassan: "Yes."

Moshe: "Now, it is time to bring up the most sensitive of issues. And that being, which I could see Hassan wanted to bring up before . . . that of the borders of Palestine and Israel and of the future of cities as Jerusalem, Ramallah, Bethlehem and so. So let us discuss that. Now I try to be fair to the Palestinian people and to the Israeli people, but it must be something the Israelis can accept. And this issue of the borders, it really is an issue of the have and the have not."

Hassan: "But, what. . . "

Moshe: "We (Israel) control all of Judea, Samaria, Gaza, and all of Jerusalem. When Jordan occupied Jerusalem, East Jerusalem, Jews were not allowed to go to the Western Wall. Garbage was thrown on the wall in spite toward our people living across the city . . . putting humiliation upon all Jews around the world! Once we conquered Jerusalem, of course we made that area ours and it has become the symbol of Israel. But we have also tried to respect the Palestinian holy sites . . . whether Christian or Muslim, as the Dome of the Rock or the Church of the Holy Sepulchre. We have not thrown garbage or defaced the walls of the Dome. We have sought to protect these areas and have allowed the Palestinians to protect them. The Islamic Waqf (the Muslim Trust) continue to administer and protect!"

Hassan: "What about the fires set in Al Aqsa (Mosque) or the Jews that want to destroy our holy areas and dominate the Harem Al Sharif?"

Moshe: "They have not been successful and will not! The Temple Mount Faithful fanatics are no better than the PLO in my eyes!

"In light of this, in light of Jerusalem having been a city settled and established by Jews, over three thousand years ago . . . we will not give up Jerusalem, period!"

Hassan: "Well, no! We're going to have quite a problem here, Moshe! My people want Jerusalem, we want East Jerusalem, it has to be part of us. Part of the historical and religious significance of Palestine . . . is Jerusalem . . . you and I both know that! Yes?"

Moshe: "I do know that, but there is no way my people will accept giving up Jerusalem again, any part of it."

Hassan: "You know this is, this is the kind of thing, it's a decision where us being one man, one man making a decision like this. Where as I may be willing to accept, but my people would kill me for making such a sacrifice. East Jerusalem must be the capital of Palestine! Even if it's very small. Jerusalem is the heart and soul of every Palestinian!"

Moshe: "My people will never bend on Jerusalem."

Hassan: "Jerusalem is part of the occupied territories and what we consider the center of our Palestinian homeland! We can never cede our ties to Jerusalem."

Moshe: "Jerusalem is our capital and we have annexed the whole of it."

Hassan: "Illegally annexed it! There is no international legitimacy to this. Security Council Resolution 242 declares East Jerusalem as part of the occupied territories that Israel must withdraw from it."

Moshe: "What we have . . . "

Hassan: "There is no . . . "

Moshe: "What we have, listen please, what we have is Jerusalem and ten kilometers around Jerusalem, around the city, will be taken and remain Israel. Not including Bethlehem. Bethlehem will be part of Palestine. But Israel will come very close. Jerusalem must be secure. The reason we go ten kilometers around is to include many of the settlements around Jerusalem . . . the Israeli settlements. I am claiming ten kilometers, approximately, because it would be farther in some areas and less in others to include the settlements. This is one situation where the religious fanatics as Tehiya control the government and there is no way we can go any other way!

"What we will do, as long as the blood between Palestinian and Israeli is good, and if it is bad, we will try to keep an open border to East Jerusalem for free passage of Palestinians, both for business and tourism. And that we will put in the treaty . . . and in the treaty the borders, of Jerusalem in particular, you will, Hassan, recognize Jerusalem as the capital and sole property of Israel! But Israel accepts and understands the importance of Jerusalem to Palestinians, Christians and Muslims and Arabs in general; and will allow Palestinians free travel, through the border, to East Jerusalem for religious and business activity. And this will be honored.

"We have bent over backward to protect the Temple Mount and those areas. The Islamic Waqf will continue to control and protect the Muslim sector of the Temple Mount. And we will continue it, but I can never, ever give up Jerusalem . . . nor would any other Israeli."

Hassan: "Well this is, you know, very very disconcerting, because I thought in this peace settlement you would probably try to give us, maybe the very eastern quarter of Jerusalem as our corner, as our capital of Palestine. It is very disconcerting . . . that you won't give way on any of it . . . "

Moshe: "There are five Jews for every one Palestinian in Jerusalem. The city has a commanding majority of Jews."

Hassan: "That is the result of your Zionist campaign of dispersing my people while settling every hillside with Jews outside the municipality of Jerusalem . . . and then you redraw the lines of the municipality to include all these Jewish settlements. Your people are warping the facts to your need. In all fairness you must relinquish part of Jerusalem to my people!"

Moshe: "I cannot!"

(Period of quiet and very tense. I thought Hassan would walk out and the conversation would end here, on a very abrupt note. Fortunately, Moshe pursued the conversation of the dialogue after nearly five minutes.)

Moshe: "Your heart speaks, but you know that I could never hand over part of Jerusalem . . . it is unrealistic . . . Tehiya and Gush Emunim would skin me alive. They would never accept such a decision."

Hassan: "Well, if it is to be this way we must have a face-saving compromise where we (the Palestinians) can still have legal rights and ties to Jerusalem."

Moshe: "What do you mean? There is no compromise on Jerusalem as Israeli territory."

Hassan: "I really have no choice but to accept. But my life may be no better than Sadat's . . . though Sadat is seen as a hero to the world, not to Arabs . . . If I accept your borders on Jerusalem there must be conditions!"

Moshe: "Such as?"

Hassan: "If Jerusalem is not part of our state, then we must have significant ties to it. There must be free passage from Palestine to East Jerusalem and to the Harem Al Sharif, under Israeli Defense Forces protection.

"But no interrogation and humiliation of my people, as is evident for any Palestinian who tries to enter Israel today.

"Palestinians of Jerusalem are allowed full-Israeli citizenship and protection and always, be allowed full citizenship of Palestine.

So Palestinians get dual citizenship if they so chose."

Moshe: "But no taxation by Palestine on any residents of Jerusalem!"

Hassan: "Why?"

Moshe: "Because that is a crude way of saying Palestine has control of East Jerusalem."

Hassan: "I see . . . that is acceptable. There are a few additional conditions. The Islamic Waqf continues to administer and control the holy areas of Harem Al Sharif, but will be given more power to protect it, with weapons if necessary, to protect against the Jewish extremists as Meir Kahanes' Kach movement who seek to destroy this holy of places."

Moshe: "The weapons will be limited! But IDF support will be extended, if you think necessary."

Hassan: "The abuses of Palestinians in East Jerusalem will cease! No more house demolition, no more land confiscation, no midnight interrogations, no more rampant taxation, no forcing out Palestinians who choose to remain in Jerusalem! In sum, all Palestinians will be treated equally as Jews by the state and police. And those that don't will be punished!

"Palestinians of East Jerusalem will be allowed to use the Palestinian currency as well as yours. Citizens of Palestine will be allowed work in East Jerusalem, but not Israeli citizenship."

Moshe: "I accept your terms, but the important thing is for the Palestinians of Jerusalem to stop agitating and uncovering sacred rocks. Troublemakers will be jailed on both sides!

"The Palestinians of Jerusalem may have dual citizenship, but they are not allowed political position in Palestine. If they do they must immigrate permanently to Palestine or we will do it for them. In seeking office their Israeli citizenship is permanently confiscated, only to be returned by petition to the Israeli authority."

Hassan: "Agreed, but his family may remain, if he does seek position."

Moshe: "Accepted, but any man, such as Faisal Husseini, cannot seek a seat as the representative of East Jerusalem. Jerusalem is Israeli and should not be put in compromising position!"

Hassan: "Understood. Let us hear more about the borders. Wait . . . *(Hassan opened his briefcase and began thumbing through papers.)* Here it is, a detailed map of Palestine, Israel and the occupied territories. Go on. What else do you have for . . . for my Palestine?"

Moshe: "Okay, the other points I will go through slowly. The border arrangements, throughout, along the whole area of Judea, Samaria, Gaza there will be a three kilometer demilitarized dead zone. If there is a farm there now, a factory there now . . . going into Palestine, it will be destroyed, leveled, fenced, mined, electronics placed, a sand field raked continually . . . will be the border.

"There will be four border crossing points. One in the north, one in Jerusalem, one in the South, and one in Gaza. Keep it simple. The Palestinians in Jerusalem will be allowed joint citizenship. The other Arabs in Israel will not be allowed to carry Palestinian citizenship. Strictly Israeli citizenship unless they move to Palestine. The Jerusalem Arabs will be the exception . . . they can have dual citizenship, as we have agreed."

Hassan: "I can accept this."

Moshe: "The Palestinian capital cannot, by our treaty, the Palestinians, can not have your capital as Jerusalem, as Ramallah, as Bethlehem or any city near the Jerusalem area. But we encourage that your capital be Nablus or Hebron."

Hassan: "Yes, I can say on that now, that without Jerusalem our capital will most definitely be Hebron. We don't want it in Gaza or Nablus. Hebron is a great historical city for us. Hebron, where the prophet Abraham and Sarah are buried, it will be the capital of Palestine. I think we can settle that now. Also, Hebron will be in the middle of our country . . . nearest to Gaza."

Moshe: "I think that is ideal. The point I want to bring up . . ."

Hassan: "The other thing I think I should say now that we are discussing the borders . . . we're going to have the Gaza and the West Bank . . . there is no connection between the two, though. What we want is to have some sort of corridor between the Gaza and West Bank or permission to fly over . . . "

Moshe: "Absolutely not! There will no flights over Israel by Palestinians!"

Hassan:"What do you mean, no? We must have connection between our peoples. What, okay, if there is going to be no flights we want a corridor . . . a corridor from Gaza to Hebron. A corridor straight through Israel where we can have a highway, a four-lane highway, and several train tracks. All fenced in or whatever you need, but we must have a corridor. Modeled on maybe that of the corridor through East Germany that linked West Germany to West Berlin. I had not seen it myself, but I am told it worked well."

Moshe: "That I accept. That is something I have spent much time thinking on. Israelis will build the corridor and Arab labor will be needed. The corridor will go along this path, winding through the hills, will be fenced in, will be mined around it, you will have several petrol stops in the corridor. There must never be any deviation from this corridor! There will be no exits, there will be several petrol stops and help stops, but there must be no attempts at getting off the track. A straight corridor going through, but the important thing here is it is up to Palestinian security that this corridor is not misused. No terrorists . . . no jumping off their cars with their Kalashnikov's and sneaking into Israel! No military equipment must go through . . . nothing of that nature! Because you, the Palestinians, must have border checks and make sure this is not abused in the least. If the corridor is abused and used for terrorist activity the corridor will be closed permanently and the only way to connect the two will be a flight all the way around Israel over Sinai or up over Lebanon and around. And we both know you'd not want to do that. Because of the corridor . . . we will build it and set up the security and we will monitor from the air and land. But it is up to you to make sure it is not abused."

Hassan: "We can accept that! I think it would be up to us anyway. I mean we want to do all the security, we don't want to have any Jewish interference on the corridor and we will work to make certain that it is never used in any type terrorist, launch ground. I give my word on this."

Moshe: "Next on . . . you are going to want, brings up airspace. There will be no air travel allowed over Israeli territory or within fifteen kilometers of Israeli territory. That is firm! We do not want to see any planes, any planes near Israeli airspace because our airforce will be up and will destroy them before they get close. That . . . being to avoid disaster. Additionally if you look on this map, I am drawing a line nearly ten kilometers into Palestine that is Israeli airspace. We can fly over these lands any time we chose . . . to view and survey the conditions below."

Hassan: "It must be high altitude flights that do not antagonize our people!"

Moshe: "It is our decision."

Hassan: "Let us say no flights lower than ten thousand meters and only for two years after the occupation forces withdraw."

Moshe: "All I will say is nothing lower than two thousand meters . . . unless we have reason to look lower. As long as the borders are silent there will be no problem with this . . . and with no time limit."

Hassan: "Okay."

Moshe: "What we suggest is, you are going to want to build the airport, or maybe two airports. What we could suggest is have your international airport along the Dead Sea here . . . either in the area of Jericho or farther south, closer to your capital (Hebron). No flights cross Israeli territory! If you want to have another international airport on the coast of Gaza, fine. But no flights ever shall cross Israel or any flights within fifteen kilometers of Israel. We have control of ten kilometers of your airspace and five kilometers will be a dead zone.

"In addition, international waters will be respected along the coasts . . . so no airplanes should come near the coast of Israel. What we are interested in here is security. This will prevent any unwanted accidents or anything that could hurt both of our peoples."

Hassan: "I agree."

Moshe: "So, look at the map. One airport here (on the Dead Sea) and one airport here (Gaza coast). All flights go out this way . . . so over water or out over Jordan. You must get Hussein's approval on flight paths out of this airport. No exceptions over Israel."

Hassan: "I believe the King will help us with this."

Moshe: "If not, do not have this airport, use the Gaza airport or travel to the Amman airport . . . it is close."

Hassan: "Well that is true, but we do not want to depend on anyone again! What if we have a flight corridor from here (Dead Sea) to here (Red Sea) on the Israeli-Jordan border?"

Moshe: "No! Absolutely no!"

Hassan: "But why?"

Moshe: "Too close of contact is asking for problems. That border is often flown by our airforce and is asking for a problem."

Hassan: "You are not flexible on this?"

Moshe: "No!"

Hassan: "What we really must have is, cooperation so that no accidents can happen and I think this is very good . . . I mean I am listening to you giving me what we have to do, but I understand the way it has to be for you and your people. But I think as carefully, and am as preoccupied with security as we can be to prevent any accidents. There will be no justification for either the Jews or the Palestinian people to create any type of warring situation. That's what we want."

Moshe: "Yes, agreed."

Hassan: "Okay."

Moshe: "Obviously you can have seaports on Gaza, manmade ports and that type of thing, but it is up to you, and I am sure you will want one. But what I must stress is that all ships steer clear of Israeli waters. We prefer additional twenty kilometers into international waters for Palestinian shipping . . . and an additional twenty kilometers for airplanes at sea."

Hassan: "As long as our shipping is in international waters!"

Moshe: "Again, I am trying to prevent problems! We patrol our waters closely . . . by sea and air . . . for potential terrorists, as from Lebanon. If a Palestinian ship crosses into Israeli waters, accidentally or not, or is very close, our airforce may fire . . . thus causing an international incident and increasing conflict with Palestine.

"In our treaty let us sign that Palestinian shipping will stay an additional twenty kilometers off Israeli waters, unless emergency signals have been received. If no emergency signal is seen and a Palestinian boat is near our water, she will be fired on! We will not wait to see if it is an attack on Tel Aviv or elsewhere."

Hassan: "That is not a problem, with the exception of shipping to Lebanon."

Moshe: "You agree then?"

Hassan: "Yes, except for this area on the border (Gaza, Palestine and Israel). Here, straight out, let us make it five kilometers. The whole length of Gaza is hardly twenty kilometers!"

Moshe: "Okay, five kilometers here, twenty kilometers here, and twenty kilometers here."

Hassan: "Yes, and it should be the same for Israeli shipping near Gaza. Five kilometers and twenty kilometers . . . outside our waters. Agree?"

Moshe: "Yes, but will our generals agree? As for mineral rights, water rights we want them to be fairly sold to Israel . . . just as we will fairly sell our products to you. We use much water from the Jordan and the water tables under Samaria. We have access to it on our own, we could always cut off the Jordan to you, but that is not what we want. So in the treaty we want Palestine to agree to treat Israel fairly and sell us mineral and water rights, just as, because you know there are many water rights in the territories . . . the underground water Israel has been using. It is best for both of us to work together."

Hassan: "So, then, the treaty includes stipulations against altering or cutting off resources, such as the Jordan."

Moshe: "Yes. Now let us get on further to the security of creating the nation of Palestine and, how we can accept it."

Hassan: "Go on."

Moshe: "Militarily, Palestine will be set up as a neutral nation which we will state in the treaty. Meaning you will have no offensive forces. For one, there would be a demilitarized zone along the Israeli border extending ten kilometers into Palestine. Israel can have forces all along the border. Palestine must not have any forces within ten kilometers of the border. Sure, you will have your border patrols with machine guns and such, but no offensive weaponry . . . tanks, rocket launchers, anything that can be considered offensive; a demilitarized zone . . . "

Hassan: "And?"

Moshe: "Palestine will be a non-offensive nation, it will be a neutral nation to be maintained by defensive troops, or, if you so choose, you may have none. But you may not have offensive. You must not get into the problem of having men developing military strategy. Because if we start receiving intelligence of Palestinian military command study of incursions into Israel, into Jordan, Saudi Arabia, or Egypt, we will get nervous and start to think that Palestine is becoming an offensive nation . . . which will be a danger to Israel and our security.

"No foreign troops will be allowed in Palestine, no Arab armies or air force will be allowed in Palestine. All of this must be included in the neutrality pacts with Israel. No chemical or nuclear weapons must ever be allowed in Palestine! That would be reason for immediate reoccupation. You are a neutral nation . . . defensive forces, non-offensive . . . no air travel within twenty kilometers of Israel."

Hassan: "No, we agreed fifteen kilometers!"

Moshe: "Yes, you are correct."

Hassan: "Continue, please."

Moshe: "There must be, we must have tours of the Jordanian-Palestine border three times a year and on our request. The Palestinians will take our people, our military to the border . . . looking for offensive weaponry from Jordan."

Hassan: "Well, no, I don't think we should have any type of, of mixing of that nature, military. As Palestinians we cannot be seen, many Arabs would see us as Zionists. Many Arab countries see Zionists as anyone in aid of you . . . we will also be seen as the enemy. We cannot have that and we do not want that. We know you Israelis . . . you have both your own satellites and access to Washington's intelligence resources. You will be able to see what type of military movements are happening."

Moshe: "That is a fair point and I think we want, I know there are many military men in my nation that are to want access to those areas."

Hassan: "Well, it's not, it is unacceptable, because we cannot be seen as a Jewish stooge in the Arab world. I don't mean that in an offensive way, but if we're seen as a Zionist stooge, Palestine as just an Israeli puppet government . . . we are dead! These other Arab governments will attack our government from within and we cannot have revolution and that type of thing. Because it will be tragedy for you and I."

Moshe: "This point is accepted and I agree . . . But what I am saying there is, we will try to share intelligence in terms of both nations security. If we pick up something that the Syrians are trying to destabilize Palestine we will put that information forward. Just as we expect you to do the same if Syrian, Lebanese involvement is seen aligned against Israel for military incursion."

Hassan: "I agree, that is, we should put that in our treaty, we try sharing intelligence at the protection of each other as brotherly states."

Moshe: "It is accepted. Now, those are really the main points that I have worked through on how I see peaceful coexistence."

Day Two

Hassan: "I think there are some very important points we have not yet touched on, and I'm sure to leave here with many others that I haven't even considered. But the thing that comes to mind . . . we will have a Palestinian state . . . note, stop, stop, you know in these discussions we went over the borders but we did not go over the borders in detail. We should go over those borders or are we going to honor the Green Line border?"

Moshe: "No, no, no . . . I am pleased you brought that up because I forgot to address that point. Let me get that map again and sketch it now. Because I, there are some things that cannot be that you will not be happy with, Hassan. But it is the way it has to be. I am pleased you remembered this because we would have to discuss the border at some point, regardless. The Green Line means nothing, it is history."

Hassan: "Let us get on with it."

Moshe: "Now, if you look at the map like I said, around Jerusalem it will be ten kilometers average radius round and at some points it will be a bit farther to include settlements. So at the furthest point it, I think, that I have looked at a map on Jerusalem, we've got nearly thirteen kilometers and at the shortest seven kilometers. Bethlehem, Ramallah and those areas will not be included . . . those will be Palestine."

Hassan: "I should hope so!"

Moshe: "Like I said before there will be free travel from East Jerusalem for Arabs, Palestinian Arabs primarily. In addition, there are some other points we will not allow to be part of Palestine. Now if you look here . . . you see this peninsula on the West Bank, of Latrun that includes the main roads from Tel Aviv to Jerusalem. Now that is not to be part of Palestine! The whole peninsula, from here, along this path, including Beit Sira, Beit Liqya, Qubeiba will be Israel permanently . . . all the way to near, Ramallah. Those people are welcome to remain, welcome to sell their property to Israelis, and move, but that will be a permanent part of Israel.

"And here also . . . south of Jerusalem to Bethlehem."

Hassan: "No! . . . This is, you know, we cannot have you dividing up our state. You've allowed us a very small state as it is and we don't want it chopped up. This agreement must carry international legitimacy to the Palestinian people!" How am I to go to these families and tell them . . . they will not be part of Palestine?"

Moshe: "I understand that, but security is primary and Jerusalem can never be cut off now, because it is already in there, (pointing to map) we cannot take the risk of it being closed off . . . by road."

Hassan: "You didn't have a problem with security pre-1967 with only half of Jerusalem!"

Moshe: "Maybe so, but times have changed and so have the weaponry available to terrorists."

Hassan: "Okay, okay!"

Moshe: "Along this Jerusalem area you see seven to thirteen kilometers in there. If we look up here to, to Tulkarm and Qalqiliya there is a little area of the region that will be taken for Israel . . . in the north this small area here, and here and along the Jordan will be taken. In the south there are some areas where there is not much settlement, but we are going to keep part of it, because we are going to give you the corridor and we are going to build that corridor. So we are going to take part of this desolate area. This here and along here."

Hassan: "Write with your pencil."

Moshe: "In Gaza . . . only a small area here . . . as a buffer to Tel Aviv."

Hassan: "Where else?"

Moshe: "Other than that it will be Judea, Samaria, Gaza and the corridor. Let us draw it here, where the corridor will go . . . the corridor will go across here. Our engineers will work out the details to the route."

*(Please see maps after Chapter 6 for details on the borders
of Palestine.)*

Hassan: "I don't know! You know, I mean, I find this unacceptable but I have to accept. You are cutting off parts of
Palestine and Palestinian homelands. I have to answer to my
people for this agreement."

Moshe: "Listen, it is either this or we have nothing. You
understand that Jerusalem cannot come under risk, that is why
these areas are being trimmed."

Hassan: "I must say, I understand, I understand, you Jews
are so preoccupied with security, its . . . I'm sorry Moshe,
please continue."

Moshe: "Other than that . . . all of Judea, Samaria, Gaza, the
corridor, your capital in Hebron, the airports . . . and I think your
nation has a beginning . . .

"But your people will no longer be allowed to use Jerusalem
and our road system as a transit point. You will need to build a
vehicle road system around Israeli territory. Jerusalem is open to
Palestinians, but not as a bus station."

Hassan: "Security I'm sure is your reason, once again!"

Moshe: "Yes it is."

Hassan: "That is okay. As soon as we have independence I
will propose a detailed transit system . . . a large paved roadway,
alongside a set of train tracks along this route.

"From Nablus, cutting through here, if it can be engineered,
to Jericho, to our capital Hebron, and then through the corridor
to Gaza and to our seaport for import and export trade. Train
extensions and roads will come from Jenin and Tulkarm to the
Nablus train station. From Ramallah a line to Jericho station, and
from Bethlehem a line to Hebron. From Khan Yunis, a line to
Gaza. This will connect our state by railway and road . . . for our
people to travel, and more importantly for business and trade.

"Also a line from Khan Yunis to the Egyptian border and a
line from Jericho to the Jordanian border."

Moshe: "You have thought much about this!"

Hassan: "Yes . . . a good transportation system is central to commerce. We also must have a railway line from Hebron and Jericho to our international airport on the Dead Sea. Additionally, a line from Gaza to our airport there. We want a rail line to East Jerusalem someday for our people. Easy access will benefit all of us."

Moshe: "That is doubtful . . . for some time to come."

Hassan: "We will connect a line from Jericho to Bethlehem along our border here . . . and along the paths of all railways we will build a sister road for the bus and automobile."

Moshe: "You are very optimistic on the potential of your people."

Hassan: "Quite! And rightfully so."

Moshe: "I commend you, your rail system plans look impressive . . . if it works."

Hassan: "Yes, it looks good, it's something I can take pride in, if my people accept my transportation plan. There are other issues we must address here."

Moshe: "More than we know."

Hassan: "The most important issue that I—not the most important, but one of the most important issues is the Jewish settlers in the territories. You addressed it yourself, it's these radical extremist Zionist groups that are continually waging battle against Palestinians. And it creates a very unwanted situation of bad will. The Jewish settlers must be removed from Palestine! With well over one-hundred and fifty Jewish settlements in the occupied lands with such people as Levinger at Kiryat Arba, there can never be peace."

Moshe: "Then you are saying if we withdraw, if we remove these Jews from Palestine, then we should expect you to remove all Palestinians from Jerusalem and elsewhere in Israel?"

Hassan: "No, no, no, no! This is a drastically different situation I'm afraid. The Palestinians lived in those areas of Israel, in

Jerusalem and so forth. They have rights to those lands . . .
they've lived there for a very long time, generations in fact.

"The Jewish settlers are the extremist religious groups to
which even you are hostile. They've moved into these areas
illegally and created these monsters *(referring to the physical
settlements themselves)* once these areas were occupied in 1967.
It is not their land, they do not deserve it. But more importantly,
it is a great risk to both of us and to our peoples. If they
continue to occupy these areas, continue to try and settle these
holy areas . . . Samaria and Judea as you call them. It will
end in conflict, there is no doubt in my mind. At some point
a Palestinian will kill a Jewish settler or a Jewish settler will
kill a Palestinian. The Israelis, as Sharon or Eitan, just looking
for a reason will enter militarily to protect these people. We've
all studied history and we know that is exactly what Hitler
did . . . entering Czechoslovakia so as to protect the persecuted
Germans in that area . . . and so too the Jews will do. We
cannot have that, that is very important . . . these Jewish settlers
must be removed!"

Moshe: "I, you have a good point. It is disturbing nonethe-
less, because like I said these Haredi parties have a great influence in Israel and to remove their followers from these areas will
be very hurtful. I agree with you the settlers must be removed
from the administered territories. But I fear doing it. I had hoped
Palestine would keep them! (ha! ha!)"

Hassan: "We'd prefer something a bit more neighborly."

Moshe: "Sure".

Hassan: "And in turn we want those settlements to remain.
They've been an eyesore for Palestinians, but we want them to
be places where we can relocate people from the refugee camps,
where Palestinians from Israel can go live. Where the refugee
camp people from Lebanon, Syria, Jordan can have a home in
Palestine . . . we must use those facilities."

Moshe: "That is acceptable, but your people may want to
burn them."

Hassan: "Indeed! . . . We want their removal quickly. When I say quickly I mean I think that, once the Palestinian government is formed, treaties are signed, all the settlers should be physically removed by Israeli military. They cannot be there when the Israeli military pulls out. Because then we'll have to go in and push out the settlers and there is sure to be blood spilled."

Moshe: "Once again, you have a point. I agree and accept that. All our settlers will be removed by the time we withdraw . . . two years after the transitional government is formed! . . . the thought of removing over seventy thousand settlers by force is not pleasing. There will be bloodshed between Jews!"

Hassan: "You must begin housing preparation for them in Israel now . . . no excuses will be accepted. They must be out by the time the occupation ends."

Moshe: "True. The Russian immigration has been difficult enough. Now another seventy thousand or so fanatics! Oye!"

Hassan: "You do have a problem . . . and the number of settlers is over one-hundred thousand!. . . "

Moshe: "One other point I must mention is in the area of refugees. When we sign formal peace treaties the Palestinian government will sign on behalf, and as the sole representative, of all the Palestinian people. The PLO will be effectively powerless . . . Your government takes the international legitimacy you request . . .

"And in the peace treaty you will sign that all Palestinian claims to land in Israel or for financial compensation for land lost in earlier wars, cease to be. All compensation issues are for the Palestinian government to handle. Israel is allowed a permanent immunity to such issues, forth."

Hassan: "The Jews have never acknowledged these claims and requests and I did not imagine you would now."

Moshe: "Good."

Hassan: "One important issue is that of Palestinian laborers in Israel. Will laborers be allowed work in Israel?"

Moshe: "Would you want them to?"

Hassan: "No, I think not, but many of these people are dependent on this work. Over forty percent of our labor force is employed in Israel. You've done a grand job devastating our economy."

Moshe: "The job of your transition government will be to put these people to work in your nation. Our job will be to replace our Arab labor with our new Russian immigrants . . . but they do not want this work. It is a problem for us also."

Hassan: "Let us agree that Palestinian laborers from the occupied territories may continue to work in Israel up to one year after the transitional government is formed. After that period each laborer will have to request Palestinian and Israeli permits. Likewise, a Jew who wants to work in Palestine must request worker permits from the Palestinian authorities. The permits will be limited in number after one year. The exception will be the citizens of Palestine that have work in East Jerusalem . . . is this acceptable?"

Moshe: "Agreed. The process must be careful to transfer the Palestinian dependence on a newly formed Palestinian economy."

Hassan: "In light of this, Palestinian investment from abroad to build the economy . . . through companies and industries that employ Palestinians, should be allowed once the transitional government is in place."

Moshe: "Acceptable, but the Israeli authorities will be monitoring for PLO or unfriendly destabilizing influences."

Hassan: "PLO financial aid must not be hampered . . . we need these funds to build an infrastructure. As the money is used for good, do not, please do not make trouble over it."

Moshe: "Then there is no problem. If the money is used to put Israelis at risk then there is a problem. Be very careful."

Hassan: "In addition, you, we've discussed establishing these peace treaties with the language of brotherly states. Brother states relying on each other, trying to help each other . . . to build this great state of Palestine. We should set up a series of goodwill agreements where we help each other. Such as goodwill agreements for tourism between our states, honored, helped, and supported by both governments. So that understanding begins to develop between our peoples. The animosity that exists now must be put to bed. In addition, I think that we should have building projects in which we work together as goodwill projects. We need Jewish technical assistance in aiding such projects as airports, maybe a seaport, harbor. We'd like to have goodwill agreements where Israelis come to work with us. In addition, we want Israel to build projects that Palestinians can come work with, even as just a monument, for friendship between Palestine and Israel. Some type of agreement where we can begin building up a brotherly feeling between us. Hard to imagine though!

"After all, you know, we both know that Jews and Palestinians in the past got along quite well before the Zionist movement began. In fact, you know, throughout the Arab nation, our Jews were treated much better by us Arabs than by your Western friends . . . the Christians. Look at what the Germans and Spanish have done to their Jews. We treated you much better here. We want to recreate that era of good feeling between Jews and Palestinians . . . where we consider ourselves brother states. Two small states, in a vast Middle East supporting each other for our very survival and existence . . . in a very hostile neighborhood."

Moshe: "First, we are not your Jews or anyone else's!"

Hassan: "I don't. . . "

Moshe: "It is okay . . . you have shown good judgement on that and we would have to take much discussion on what type of goodwill projects we could do for each other. Accidents, security accidents, could happen, but I think that certain things, goodwill agreements where Israelis provide technical expertise and help build airports and seaports, would be more than welcomed. For several reasons. The agreements would help us and it gives us a good look at these facilities for our security purposes . . . so that it shows you are not concealing anything from us. I think that is good . . . many of my people will not want to do anything to help you . . . so we will see."

Hassan: "You know, I think this settlement is a positive development for the peace process . . . and, I think Israel has been a successful state, but spends too much on the military. I understand why, but do you? I think you will be straddled alongside a very successful Palestinian state. You know, what we are to do, is we are going to have a focus on agriculture and we plan to develop a main industry. Not just oranges in Gaza! We're going to develop an industry. And it would be good if both Palestinians and Israelis can work together.

"We're going to receive much investment from abroad, but we won't accept Jewish investment. We made that mistake once before. You won't accept Palestinian investment into Israel, most likely. But we want it to be a very successful Palestinian state, we have many successful people . . . if we put our energies together to build a successful state the world will be dumbfounded.

"We will want to work with, how should I say . . . joint ventures between the Palestinian and Israeli companies to develop industries at which we can be successful, such as exporting to Europe and the Arab world. Our goal must be two successful, peaceful states, of Israel and Palestine. I think that is in our future.

"I must say, Moshe, I find you to be much more flexible in your goals for Palestine-Israel than I imagined . . . with the exception of Jerusalem. I thought we would probably not agree on a thing . . . but I don't think you gave away the house."

Moshe: "I like your vision, Hassan, but I am not as optimistic as you! I make this peace out of need for my people. My greatest fear is a real risk, that your Palestine could become another Lebanon. If that happens the extremists will have you all in refugee camps in Jordan and Lebanon!"

Hassan: "Sharon and his cronies will pay someday! . . . You know, you're not like the man I remember you to be."

Moshe: "I don't remember meeting before."

Hassan: "Well, you probably would not recall, but, like I said, I come from Nablus, and I do remember you at the military administration in Nablus. Am I right, where you there?"

Moshe: "Yes, in, I believe 1974 and 1975."

Hassan: "I myself had no problem with you, but I tried to help my neighbors and family who did have problems. Which I'm sure you remember. Nablus was not a pretty site, not a pretty site now either. Tensions are very high. The Intifada will not die, it is in the heart of my people!"

Moshe: "It is late and I must be going. Although this discussion will have little effect on the peace process it does prove to me that we do have hope!"

George: "I want to thank both of you for agreeing to participate in this dialogue, especially in such a tense time."

Hassan: "I am pleased to have been a part of this. Let us hope peace can be achieved. At this stage it is jihad or peace! My people have reached the point of complete desperation. The Intifada will go on . . . it is in the heart of our young. If Allah (God) is willing, peace will come."

Coming To Terms With Oneself
by Jorge (Mullen) - 1994 oil on canvas

Chapter 9

Conclusion

"Who dares nothing, need hope for nothing." —Schiller

Moshe and Hassan succeeded in developing an Israeli-Palestinian peace agreement because they were willing to make the difficult compromises and sacrifices. Partial compromises and partial sacrifices serve only as half-solutions that will not result in a lasting settlement. Half-solutions are those which try to appease both peoples, but never really resolve the issues. In essence, the issues are left in limbo. Unfortunately, half-solutions are the standard arguments emanating from the diplomats and educators in their effort to end this conflict. Examples being the arguments for Palestinian autonomy instead of statehood, for a Palestinian confederation with Jordan instead of an independent Palestine, for allowing the Jewish settlers to remain in the occupied territories instead of withdrawing them, for the Israeli Defense Forces (IDF) to hold positions in the occupied territories instead of withdrawal, for Jerusalem to be the capital of both Israel and Palestine instead of solely Israel, for the establishment of an autonomous Palestinian district and a free trade zone in Jerusalem instead of one government governing the entire city.

These half-solutions, along with the others, may initially be appealing, but will eventually come back to haunt both peoples, for issues that are not clearly resolved will fester and resurface.

This book recommends implementing the difficult and unpopular choices that will resolve the controversial issues of concern. These include statehood for the Palestinians, the withdrawal of the Israeli Defense Forces (IDF) and the Jewish settlers from the occupied territories, and the affirmation of Jerusalem as the capital and territory of Israel alone. Although these hard choices will be difficult and distasteful to many, they will finally leave both peoples with a clear knowledge of where they stand. No issues will be left unanswered or in limbo. Neither the Israelis nor the Palestinians will be able to reopen these resolved issues. If they do, they will be promoting an action of injustice that could negate their legitimacy as a state.

Though a small part of the Middle East, Israel-Palestine plays a major role in its affairs. Jews, Muslims, and Christians alike have significant religious and historical ties to this holy land. The uncompromising positions that are preventing peace are few, but formidable. It is time to put the history of Israel-Palestine behind us and move forward with making the future better. Israel's future is linked to the future of the Palestinians and vice versa. When one suffers so will the other, and when one prospers so will the other.

The recent PLO recognition of Israel's right to exist, Israel's acknowledgment of the PLO as the legitimate representative of the Palestinian people, and the Gaza-Jericho First Autonomy Plan are the beginning steps toward a lasting peace settlement. It is time for the Israeli and Palestinian leaders to make the necessary sacrifices and compromises. The children of Israel and Palestine deserve a future based on brotherhood, justice, and peace.

Selecteb Bibliography

Albright, Joseph, and Marcia Kunstel. *Their Promised Land*. New York: Crown Publishers, Inc., 1990.

Bill, James A., and Carl Leiden. *Politics in the Middle East*. Boston: Little Brown & Company, 1984.

Binur, Yoram. *My Enemy, My Self*. New York: Penguin, 1990.

Chacour, Elias. *We Belong to the Land*. New York: Harper San Francisco, 1990.

Cohen, Michael. *Palestine and the Great Powers 1945 - 1948*. Princeton, N.J.: Princeton University Press, 1982.

Friedman, Thomas L. *From Beirut to Jerusalem*. New York: Farrar, Straus & Giroux, 1989.

Fromkin, David. *A Peace to End All Peace*. New York: Avon Books, 1989.

Gibb, H.A.R. *Mohammedanism*. London: Oxford Press, 1969.

Glubb, Sir John. *A Short History of the Arab Peoples*. New York: Dorset Press, 1969.

Hadawi, Sami. *Bitter Harvest*. New York: Olive Branch Press, 1989.

Hart, Alan. *Arafat*. London: Sidgwick & Jackson Limited, 1984.

Heller, Mark A., and Sari Nusseibeh. *No Trumpets, No Drums*. New York: Hill & Wang, 1991.

Herzog, Chaim. *The Arab-Israeli Wars*. New York: Vintage, 1984.

Hurwitz, J.C. *The Struggle for Palestine*. New York: W.W. Norton, 1950.

Jaffee Center for Strategic Studies. *The West Bank and Gaza: Israeli's Options for Peace*. Tel Aviv: Tel Aviv University, 1989.

Kinross, Lord. *The Ottoman Centuries*. New York: Morrow Quill Paperbacks, 1977.

Lacquer, Walter, and Barry Rubin, eds. *The Israeli-Arab Reader, A Documentary History of the Middle East Conflict*. New York: Penguin, 1969.

Lamb, David. *The Arabs*. New York: Random House, Inc., 1987.

Machiavelli, Niccolo. *The Prince and the Discourses*. New York: Random House, Inc., 1940.

Mackey, Sandra. *Lebanon*. New York: Congdon & Weed, Inc., 1989.Mansfield, Peter. *The Arabs*. New York: Penguin, 1985.

Mattar, Philip. *The Mufti of Jerusalem*. New York: Columbia University Press, 1988.

Neff, Donald. *Warriors at Suez*. New York: The Linden Press/Simon & Schuster, 1981.

Sadat, Anwar el. *In Search of Identity*. New York: Harper Colophon Books, 1979.

Seale, Patrick. *Asad*. Berkeley: University of California Press, 1988.

Segal, Jerome M. *Creating the Palestinian State*. Chicago: Lawrence Hill Books, 1989.

Shakir, M.H. *The Qur'an*. New York: Tahrike Tarsile Qur'an, Inc., 1988.

Shipler, David K. *Arab and Jew*. New York: Times Books, 1986.

Shlaim, Avi. *Collusion Across the Jordan: King Abdullah, the Zionist Movement and the Partition of Palestine*. New York: Columbia University Press, 1988.

Smith, Pamela Ann. *Palestine and the Palestinians 1876 - 1983*. New York: St. Martin's Press, 1984.

Stein, Kenneth. *The Land Question in Palestine, 1917 - 1939*. Chapel Hill, N.C.: University of North Carolina Press, 1984.

Wilson, Mary. *King Abdullah, Britain and the Making of Jordan*. Cambridge: Cambridge University Press, 1987.

Wynn, Wilton. *Nasser of Egypt*. Cambridge: Arlington Books, Inc., 1959.

Index

Airport, 34, 38, 85-86, 93, 97

Abbas, Abul, 7

Abdullah, Crown Prince of Saudi Arabia, 78

Abdullah Ibn Hussein, King of Jordan, 61

Abraham, 1, 13, 83

Al-Aqsa Mosque, 3, 35, 79

Al-Fajr, ix

Al-Fatah, 5, 53

Alexander, The Great, 2

Amman, 86

Apartheid, 19, 20

Arab League, 5

Arafat, Yasir, 5-8, 49, 53, 59, 60, 67-69, 71

Assad, Hafez Al, 7, 75, 77

Assyrians, 2

Babylonians, 2

Baghdad, 27

Bar Kochba revolt, 3

Begin, Menachem, 6, 59

Beit Liqya, 90

Beit Sira, 90

Ben-Gurion, David, 48

Bethlehem, 78, 80, 83, 90, 91, 93

Brooklyn, New York, 12

Bush, George, 16

Byzantine Empire, 3, 13

Canaanites, 1
Canada, 20
Confederation, with Jordan, 26-27
Corridor, Gaza-Hebron, 34, 37, 84, 91-93
Crusaders, 3, 13
Czechoslovakia, 94

Damascus, 70
Dead Sea, 34, 38, 85, 86, 93
Deir Yassin, (Massacre), 56, 59
Dinar, Palestinian Currency, 39
Dome of the Rock, 3, 35, 79
Druse, 74

Egypt, 1, 2, 3, 5, 6, 12, 34, 78, 88
Eitan, Rafael, 57, 94
European Community, 13
Exodus, 2

Fahd, King of Saudi Arabia, 15, 78
Fahd Plan, 15
Fourteen Points (1920), 76
Fourth Geneva Convention, 25
France, 4, 5, 20, 77

Gaza/Gaza Strip, 1, 5, 8, 12, 14, 15, 26, 27, 33-34, 37-38, 50,
    58, 60-63, 66, 69, 73, 78, 83, 84-87, 92, 98
Gaza-Jericho First Autonomy Plan, 8, 12, 16, 17, 26, 48, 50,
85, 92, 93, 102
Germany, East, 19, 84
Germany, Nazi, 19, 21
Germany, West, 84
Golan Heights, 5, 6, 12, 14, 51, 62, 66, 73-74
Great Britain, 20, 21, 23
Green Line, of 1949 Armistice, 90
Gush Emunim, 81

Hamas, 13, 47
Haredi Parties, 63, 94
Harem Al Sharif, 79, 82
Hashemite, 27
Hasmonaean, 3
Hassan, ix, 53-99, 101
Hebron, 34, 37, 83, 85, 92
Herzl, Theodor, 4
Hussein Ibn Talal, King of Jordan, 5, 11, 27, 61, 77
Hussein, Saddam, 7
Husseini, Faisal, 70, 82

India, 20, 21
Inherent rights, 19, 21, 22, 25
International Law, 21, 25, 49
Intifada, 6, 22, 47, 60, 62, 64, 99
Iran, 12, 20, 77
Iraq, 7, 12, 27, 62, 71, 77
Islamic Jihad, 13, 47
Islamic Waqf (Trust), 35, 79, 80, 82
Israeli Defense Forces (IDF), 36, 53, 68, 70, 76, 82, 101

Jabril, Ahmed, 68
Jaffa, 56
Jenin, 33, 37, 92
Jericho, 8, 12, 16, 17, 26, 48, 50, 85, 92, 102
Jerusalem, 2-6, 14, 16, 17, 26, 27, 30, 33-35, 36-39, 47-51, 55, 59, 70, 78-83, 91, 93, 96, 98, 101
Jewish State, The (Herzl), 4
Jordan, 5, 11, 12, 16, 26, 27, 34, 51, 58, 61-63, 68, 74,76-78, 86, 88-89, 91, 92, 94, 98, 101
Jordan River, 1, 33, 88
Judah, 2
Judea, 62, 63, 66, 69, 73, 78, 83, 92, 94

Kach Movement, 13, 47, 82
Kahane, Meir, 62, 82

Kfar Kassem, 56
Khan Yunis, 92
King David Hotel (Jerusalem), 59
Kiryat Arba, 93

Labor Party, ix, 53, 63, 66
Latrun, 33, 91
Lebanon, 5, 6, 8, 12, 25, 57, 60-62, 68, 73, 77, 84, 87, 94
Levinger, Moshe, 93
Libya, 12
Likud Party, 49, 63, 64

Macedonians, 2
Mamluks, 3
McMahon Papers, 61
Mecca, 3
Mediterranean Sea, 34
Medina, 3
Mohammed, 3
Moshe, ix, 53, 54, 56-99, 101
Mullen theory of injustice, 19

Nablus, 53, 56, 83, 92, 98
Nasser, Gamal Abdel, 5, 60
Nebuchadnezzar, 2

Ottoman Empire, 4, 14

Palestine Economic Council (PEC), 38
Palestine Mandate, 4
Palestine National Congress (PNC), 7, 67
Palestine, State of, 15-16, 27, 33, 50-51, 61, 64, 73-74, 78,
     94-98
Peel Plan, 4
Persian, 2, 13
Persian Gulf, 7
Philistines, 2
PLO (Palestine Liberation Organization), 5, 6-8, 12, 15-17,
     22, 23, 27, 48, 50, 59, 60, 66-71, 74, 79, 95, 102

Popular Front, 59, 68, 69, 74
Ptolemaic, 2

Qalqiliya, 33, 91
Qibya, (Massacre), 56
Qubeiba, 90

Rabin, Yitzhak, 8
Ramallah, 33, 78, 83, 90, 92
Reagan Plan, 15-16
Red Sea, 78, 86
Roman, (Rome), 3, 14
Russia, 4, 13, 14, 20, 21, 69, 95, 96

Sabra Palestinian refugee camp, 56
Sadat, Anwar, 6, 11, 75, 77, 81
Saladin, 3
Samaria, 62, 63, 66, 69, 73, 78, 83, 87, 92, 94
Sargon II, 2
Saudi Arabia, 7, 12, 77, 78, 88
Segal, Jerome M., 16
Seleucid, 2
Settlers, Jewish (settlements), 15, 16, 21, 26, 36
Shamir, Yitzhak, 59, 75
Sharon, Ariel, 57, 62, 69, 75, 94, 98
Shatila Palestinian refugee camp, 56
Shekel, Israeli currency, 38
Sinai Peninsula, 5-6, 14, 53, 84
Sinai War, 5, 53, 56
Six-Day War, 5, 14, 53, 56
South Africa, 20, 21
Soviet Union, 5, 20
Spanish Inquisition, 13
Suez Canal, 5
Sykes-Picot Agreement, 4
Syria, 1, 2, 5-6, 12, 51, 62, 66, 68, 71, 74, 77, 78, 94

Tehiya Party, 63, 80, 81
Tel Aviv, 53, 87, 91

Temple Mount, 80
Temple Mount Faithful, 13, 47, 79
Tranjordan (Jordan), 4
Transitional Provisions, 35, 36, 38, 64-74
Tulkarm, 91, 92
Tunis, 6, 70
Tunisia, 6, 68

U.N. Partition Plan of 1947, 4, 47
United Nations, 4, 6, 7, 17, 35, 37, 38, 47, 48, 56, 61, 65, 69
United Nations Security Council Resolution *338*, 6, 60, 61, 65
United Nations Security Council Resolution *242*, 5, 6, 60, 61
    65, 80
United States, 5, 7, 8, 17, 20, 21, 23, 35, 69

West Bank, 1, 5, 14, 15, 26, 30, 33, 34, 43, 50, 55, 56,
    60-61, 69, 83, 90
White Paper, 4
Wilson, Woodrow, 76
World War I, 4
World War II, 4

Yom Kippur War, 6, 53

Zionism, 6, 7, 56, 75

About The Author

As neither an Arab nor a Jew, George D. Mullen is able to provide a unique look into the Israeli-Palestinian conflict from an objective and unbiased viewpoint. As a knowledgeable outsider, he is able to view the conflict without prejudice; whereas, those involved are easily swayed by the emotion of proximity. He has traveled extensively in the Middle East on many occasions and spent a great deal of time and energy discussing this conflict with those involved. He worked on several major archaeological excavations in Israel, including Caesarea Maritima and Rehovot ba-Negev. His theories and ideas for an Israeli-Palestinian peace settlement have been published in the *Al-Fajr* Palestinian weekly newspaper. He received his Bachelor of Arts degree in history from the University of Colorado-Boulder and presently is employed as associate vice president of a major Wall Street brokerage firm. Mullen is a Paul Harris Fellow and the president-elect of his community Rotary club.

Motivation...

Mullen was enticed to venture to the Middle East as part of the Israeli-American archaeological excavation of the ancient Roman city of Caesarea Maritima. The experience ultimately unleashed an intense passion within him for the region. He discovered the Mideast to be the living crossroads of man's past, present, and future. It represented to him, and Israel-Palestine in particular, the challenges to humanity, i.e., beginning versus ending; man versus land; brother versus brother; neighbor versus neighbor; love versus hate; conflict versus peace; tragedy versus tranquility; prophet versus prophet; man versus God; and life versus death.

Because of this first-hand knowledge of the Mideast and his support of both the Israeli and Palestinian peoples, Mullen boldly defends what is just and rejects what is unjust with the views and conduct of both peoples. Those qualities enabled Mullen to recognize the important issues standing in the way of Mideast peace and to offer a proposal acceptable to both sides to eliminate those issues and achieve lasting peace.

The paintings in this book are all original pieces by the author.